LINDEMANN GROUP

Peter Schiessl

Microsoft

WORD 2016
FIRST VOLUME
Training Book
with many Exercises

ISBN 979-8-864430-87-3
Print on Demand since 2016 in several editions
Translated into English (US) by Peter Schiessl
V241104 / Lindemann Group
Publisher: Lindemann BHIT, Munich
Postal address: LE/Schiessl, Fortnerstr. 8, 80933 Munich, Germany
E-Mail: post@kamiprint.de / Telefax: 0049 (0)89 99 95 46 83
© MSc. (UAS) Peter Schiessl, Munich, Germany
www.lindemann-beer.com / www.kamiprint.de

This book was created from a full installation of MS Office 2016. Deviations from
the descriptions and illustrations are possible due to a user-defined installation or
changes due to other installed software or as a result of updates.

Table of Contents

1. Preface	7

1.1 The three steps to Wordiness 7
    1.1.1 First Volume 7
    1.1.2 Second volume 7
    1.1.3 Third Volume 8
    1.1.4 Special editions 8
1.2 Word at a Glance 8

FORMATTING 9

Basic Operation, Structure of Word, Writing First Texts, Formatting and Saving as a File 9

2. Keyboard and Correction	11

2.1 An Exercise Text for Keyboard Operation 11
2.2 The Keyboard 12
    2.2.1 Left Side 12
    2.2.2 The Right Side 13
2.3 Paragraph or New Line 14
2.4 Edit Text 14

3. Save	15

3.1 The Icons for Files 15
3.2 The First Save 16
    3.2.1 Create and Select Folders 16
3.3 Folder, File Name, and File Extension 17
3.4 End Text or Word 18
3.5 About the Save 18

4. The Font Settings	19

4.1 The Select 19
    4.1.1 Selecting Goes Like This 19
    4.1.2 Select Exercise 20
4.2 Change Font 20
4.3 Highlight Color 21
4.4 Change Font Size 22
4.5 Set Font 23
4.6 The Text Color 24

5. Paragraph Settings	25

5.1 Basic Principles 25
5.2 Display Paragraph Marks 26
5.3 Alignment 27
5.4 The Paragraph Settings 28
    5.4.1 Exercise on the Paragraph Settings 29
5.5 Undo 29
5.6 Font and Paragraph Exercise 30

6. The Word Structure	31

6.1 The Program Window 31
6.2 The Status Line 31
6.3 Menus and Windows 32
6.4 Dialog Boxes 33
6.5 Mouse Clicks 33

6.6 Selection Buttons.. 34
6.7 Final Overview.. 34

7. View and Templates — 35
7.1 Shopping List Exercise.. 35
   7.1.1 Set Text.. 35
7.2 Zoom and View Type.. 36
7.3 Other Similar Texts.. 36
7.4 CD Insert Exercise... 37
   7.4.1 Save File as... 37
7.5 Template Exercise.. 37
7.6 Stroller Exercise... 38
7.7 Summary... 38

8. Multiple Texts/Windows — 39
   8.1.1 Adjust Window Size.. 40
8.2 Birthday Invitation with Page Frame................................ 41
8.3 The Scroll Bar... 43
8.4 Scroll Bar and Copy Exercise...................................... 44

SHAPES 45
Font selection, special Paragraphs, Frames and Shading 45

9. Design with Fonts — 47
9.1 A Headline... 47
9.2 Font Selection... 48
9.3 Effects with the Icons 49
9.4 Lock Font.. 50
9.5 Manuscripts... 50
9.6 The Font Manager 51
9.7 Transfer Format.. 51
9.8 Paragraph Settings Exercise....................................... 52
9.9 Indent Paragraphs... 52

10. Special Paragraphs — 53
10.1 Hanging Paragraph.. 53
10.2 The Paragraph Menu.. 54
10.3 Hanging with the Ruler 54
10.4 Listings.. 55
   10.4.1 Bullet Character.. 56
10.5 A Brief Summary... 56

11. Borders and Shading — 57
11.1 Exercise with Frames... 57
11.2 Shading.. 58
11.3 A Frame Line 59
11.4 Lines... 60
11.5 A Page Frame 60

12. Printing — 61
12.1 Settings 62
   12.1.1 Print Quality and Paper 62
   12.1.2 What should be Printed 62

13. More About Saving — 63
13.1 Copy File with "Save as"... 63

13.2 The Systematics of Saving.....................................63
13.3 Where, with the Texts?..64
13.4 Advantages of Folders 64
13.5 Automatic Saving 65
13.6 Restoration 65
13.7 Folder Exercise 66

LANGUAGE.................................67

Page setup, Hyphenation, Spell checking, Quick links, Icons.......................67

14. Page Setup, Hyphenation	69
14.1 Page Setup	69
14.2 The Hyphenation	71
14.2.1 The Hyphenation Options	72
14.2.2 The Manual Hyphenation	72
14.2.3 Separations by Hand	72

15. Spell Checker	73
15.1 The Principle	73
15.2 The Automatic Detection	73

16. Quick Modules alias AutoText	75
16.1 Define Quick Modules..	75
16.2 Insert Quick Modules and AutoText	76
16.3 The Menu	76
16.4 Another Quick Module	77
16.5 Quick Modules for Data Backup..............................	77
16.6 Alternatives to the Quick Module	78
16.7 Final Exercise	78

17. The Icons	79
17.1 With the US Keyboard..	79
17.2 Acute Accent and Grave Accent..............................	79
17.3 Insert Icons	80
17.4 The Special Fonts	81
17.5 Foreign Characters	82
17.6 The Special Characters	83
17.7 AutoCorrect	84
17.8 Language and Paragraph Exercise	84

TABLES.................................85

Tabs and Tables for Aligning Text...85

18. Tabs	87
18.1 Tabs Instead of Spacebars	87
18.2 Tabs Set..	88
18.3 Various Tabs	88
18.4 Problems with Tabs	89
18.5 Two More Exercises..	90
18.6 Superscripts	90

19. Tables — 91

19.1 Create Table.. 91
19.2 Add Columns or Rows 92
    19.2.1 Add Columns 92
    19.2.2 Add Lines 92
    19.2.3 Select Rows or Columns..................................... 92
    19.2.4 Move Rows and Columns 93
19.3 Embellish Table... 94
    19.3.1 Adjust Column Width 95
    19.3.2 Connect Cells... 96
    19.3.3 Format Colored Table 97
19.4 Additional Settings 97
    19.4.1 Define Table 97
    19.4.2 The Text Position 98
    19.4.3 Additional Input Options..................................... 99
    19.4.4 Timetable Exercise 100
19.5 Problems with Tables 100
19.6 Tabulators and Tables Exercise 101
    19.6.1 With Tabs and Line 101
    19.6.2 As a Table 101
    19.6.3 Add a Text at the bottom of the Footer.......... 101
19.7 Page Setup Exercise... 102

IN CONCLUSION........................ 103

WordArt, a Letter, the Help.. *103*

20. WordArt Special Effects — 105

20.1 Start WordArt... 105
20.2 Set WordArt 106
20.3 Colors and Shading 106
20.4 WordArt Exercise... 108
20.5 Mirror and Rotate WordArt...................................... 108

21. A Letter — 109

21.1 Sales Brands in Stock 110
21.2 The Letterhead in the Header Line 110
21.3 The Address.. 111
21.4 Insert Date.. 111
21.5 The Letter Text 112
21.6 The Footer 112
21.7 New Letters... 112
21.8 Letter by DIN 113
21.9 Preview 114

22. Index — 115
23. Overview — 119

Chapter 1

1. Preface

MS Word offers so many possibilities that you have to be particularly systematic in your training. The first volume presents the basics of word processing, including colored texts, frames, tables, and WordArt.

1.1 The three steps to Wordiness

With this three-part book series, MS Word is not only easy to learn but also easy to learn step by step. An overview of the three volumes is given below.

1.1.1 First Volume

♦ Introduction to Word, Operation and Program Structure,
♦ basic Word processing (Font and Paragraph settings),
♦ Design text with Frames, Colors, Numberings, and Enumerations,
♦ Tabs and Tables, Spell check, Hyphenation,
♦ WordArt …

Course objective: To make short texts appealing, e.g., a business letter or a birthday invitation.

1.1.2 Second volume

Advanced word processing with

♦ Style sheets, Headers, and Footers, Page Numbers,
♦ Footnotes and Endnotes e.g., for a Source List,
♦ Table of contents, Drawing, inserting Graphics,
♦ more about Tables, Search and Replace, Business Cards,
♦ Create Serial Letters and Labels.

Course objective: to effectively edit and design longer texts, e.g., an Annual Report or a three-column Circular.

1.1.3 Third Volume

Word for Specialists:

- Different Headers or Footers in a Text,
- Adjust Table of Contents, Index,
- automatic numbering, own Dictionaries,
- rational Working with Shortcuts, Macros
- Typesetting basics and standard printing knowledge,
- Live Headers, Break Up Extensive Documents ...

Course objective: Presentations or a Doctoral thesis with Index and different Headers should be perfectly designed.

1.1.4 Special editions

Serial letters are only dealt with in the second volume. Please note our special issues on Serial Letters and Labels, in which the respective subject has been compiled and expanded by additional exercises.

1.2 Word at a Glance

MS Word is an all-rounder talent. A small overview of what is possible:

- Word processing needless to say:
  - write normal Texts, e.g., a Business Letter,
  - designed Texts with Frames and Colors, such as an Ads,
  - Images can be inserted into texts or drawn in Word, for instance, to design a brochure or leaflet,
  - Arrange texts in frames arbitrarily and combine them with images.
- Serial letters and Labels:
  - Serial letters, Labels, Envelopes or Business Cards can be created in color with Graphics, Lines or Frames,
  - a Database can be created or a Standard Database (Excel...) can be used as the data source and
  - query options allow individual customization: Ms. Müller, Mr. Müller, To Mr. Müller.
- Long texts can be edited easily:
  - a table of contents or index can be created automatically,
  - Footnotes and Annotations can also be inserted, or
  - Different Headers and Footers can be set, even
  - the paper format can be changed within a Text.
  - Note: The division into small partial texts, e.g., one file per chapter, is, therefore, possible, but no longer necessary.
  - This allows you to create professional printable documents in addition to club brochures and private books.

First Part

Formatting

Basic Operation, Structure of Word,
Writing First Texts, Formatting and
Saving as a File

2. Keyboard and Correction

2.1 An Exercise Text for Keyboard Operation

You can type on the keyboard like on a typewriter. An illustration of the keyboard follows, with important keys and notes for PC input.

➢ Start Word: Windows icon (bottom left), then Word in the list of programs (at the bottom of W).

➢ Write the framed text with all errors so that they can be corrected afterward.

In contrast to the typewriter so shooooould be set in the 'Computäär' no line break by hand, because that takes over the computer. ¶

Because you can adjust the font and the design of the teext on the PC afterward according to your wishes. However, a larger font requires more space and all manually etched line breaks would be overfloaoaoawing! ¶

That's the one big advantage of the computer. The other is that any error can be aligned at any time. Instead of 'white-out' a small key tip and the erroar is eliminated. ¶

The computer needs to know which job you want to edit:

♦ That's what the cursor is used for, the blinking line in the text.

  ↳ At this point, you can write or delete letters.

Cursor

♦ In order to correct an error, the first step is to move the cursor to the error.

  ↳ The cursor can be moved with the directional keys with one letter per one line or

  ↳ move the mouse to another location: simply click at the spot.

  ↳ Then move the mouse away so that you do not confuse the mouse arrow with the cursor.

2.2 The Keyboard

2.2.1 Left Side

♦ The [Esc] key (Escape = escape) to cancel as the emergency key if you should have lost the overview, register!

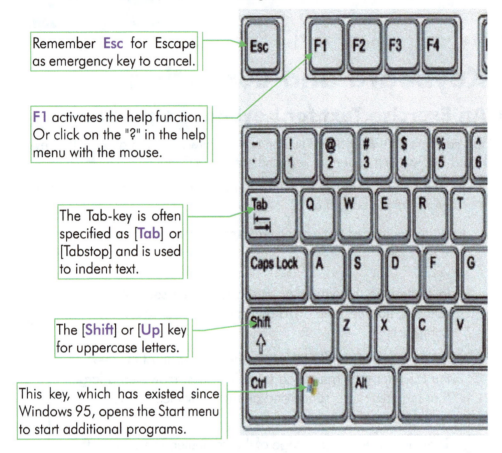

Remember Esc for Escape as emergency key to cancel.

F1 activates the help function. Or click on the "?" in the help menu with the mouse.

The Tab-key is often specified as [Tab] or [Tabstop] and is used to indent text.

The [Shift] or [Up] key for uppercase letters.

This key, which has existed since Windows 95, opens the Start menu to start additional programs.

♦ The [Shift] key (often referred to as the [Up] key) activates the upper-case letters.

  ✎ The key above is the Caps Lock key, which is used to permanently capitalize until it is pressed again.

♦ In order to be able to use keyboard shortcuts, there are two special keys on the left, [Ctrl] and [Alt],

  ✎ for example, [Ctrl]-s for Save or [Ctrl]-c for Copy.

  ✎ the [Alt] key serves the same purpose but is usually not yet assigned, so that you can use it to set up your own abbreviations (described in the second volume).

Notes: ....

....

....

....

....

....

2.2.2 The Right Side

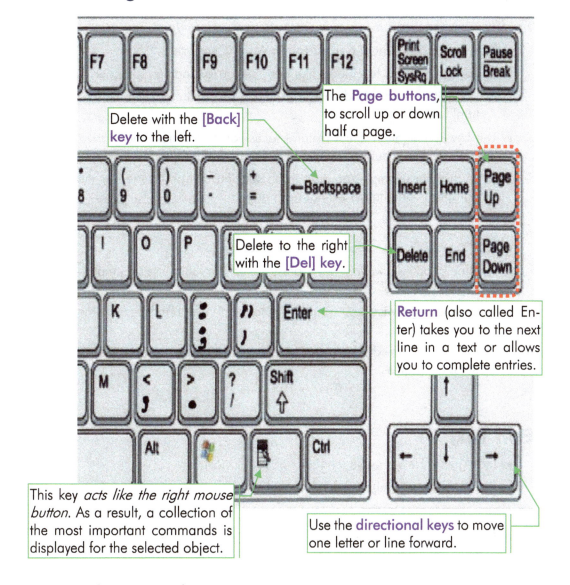

Delete with the [Back] key to the left.

The Page buttons, to scroll up or down half a page.

Delete to the right with the [Del] key.

Return (also called Enter) takes you to the next line in a text or allows you to complete entries.

This key *acts like the right mouse button.* As a result, a collection of the most important commands is displayed for the selected object.

Use the directional keys to move one letter or line forward.

Other important keys:

♦ The [Num] key (for numeric, to the right of the numbers) activates the separate number field to the right.

   ✎ Pay attention to the indicator light over Num, with these, you can write numbers, if not, the arrows apply.

♦ The [Alt Gr] key (to the right of the space bar) can be used to write the special characters ² ³ | { [ ] } @ | µ ~ printed in small letters on the keyboard.

♦ The function keys F1 to F12 are assigned functions in some programs or computer games. A selection:

   ✎ F1   Start Help or Office Assistant.

   ✎ F7   Select the Spelling command (Check Menu).

   ✎ F8   Extend the marking with the directional keys.

   ✎ F12   Select the Save As command (otherwise at File).

Keyboards are not always constructed identically. Often additional keys are available or keys are omitted to make the keyboards especially handy.

2.3 Paragraph or New Line

The following keys are particularly important (see illustration):

♦ [Return] creates a **new paragraph** in Word (Character: ¶).

    ↳ **Paragraphs** are text blocks like this one you're reading right now. ¶

    ↳ In addition, **commands** and **inputs** can be confirmed with the [Return] key. ¶

♦ The key combination [Shift]-[Return] takes you to the next line (=**new line, character**), but you remain in the same paragraph,

    ↳ so that, for example, no paragraph spacing can be inserted or the paragraph orientation cannot be changed. ¶

> This is a **paragraph** with two lines.

♦ The **line break** is done by the computer for us!!! ¶

    ↳ Simply continue writing, never press [Return] or [Shift]-[Return] manually at the end of each line, ¶

    ↳ because otherwise, you would have to reset these breaks every time you change the font size! ¶

    ↳ Manual **line feed** is only required in special cases, for example, to enter an address. ¶

2.4 Edit Text

♦ [Back] key: Delete to the left (Back or Backspace).

♦ [Delete] key (or Del): Delete to the right.

➢ Please try all variants after entering the text and correct the errors.

> The [Backspace] key deletes the left character (in the direction of the arrow!).

> The [Del] key deletes to the right.

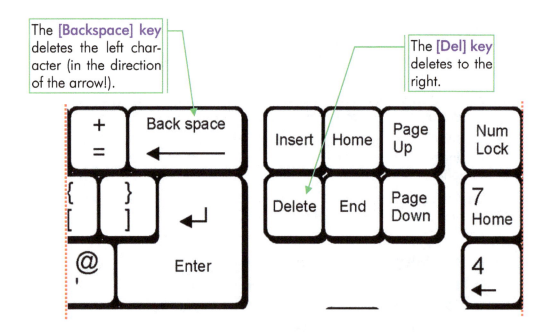

3. Save

You have already written your second text and have already set it correctly. Now it is high time to **save** this text.

3.1 The Icons for Files

All frequently used commands are displayed in Word as on-screen symbols. These symbols, also called Icons and can be clicked directly.

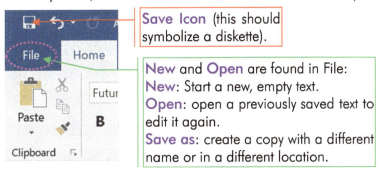

Save Icon (this should symbolize a diskette).

New and **Open** are found in File:
New: Start a new, empty text.
Open: open a previously saved text to edit it again.
Save as: create a copy with a different name or in a different location.

♦ The following keyboard shortcuts are available as an alternative:
  ↳ **[Ctrl]-n**: Start new text,
  ↳ **[Ctrl]-o**: Open existing text and
  ↳ **[Ctrl]-s**: save current text.

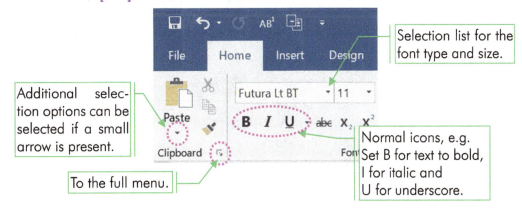

Selection list for the font type and size.

Additional selection options can be selected if a small arrow is present.

To the full menu.

Normal icons, e.g. Set B for text to bold, I for italic and U for underscore.

♦ **Info text** to the icons:
  ↳ Do not move the mouse on an icon: the meaning of the icon is displayed after a short time.
  ↳ If you move the mouse to the other icons, their meaning is also displayed.

3.2 The First Save

The error text is still open. This text should be saved on a data carrier, e.g., the hard disk.

> Select the Save Icon "Disk".

3.2.1 Create and Select Folders

> Next, the storage location should be selected, e.g., online on OneDrive or locally on your computer. Select "Browse" and the following menu will open to specify the storage location.

The computer does not yet know where the new text will be saved and what its name will be. So, the computer asks you with the following window:

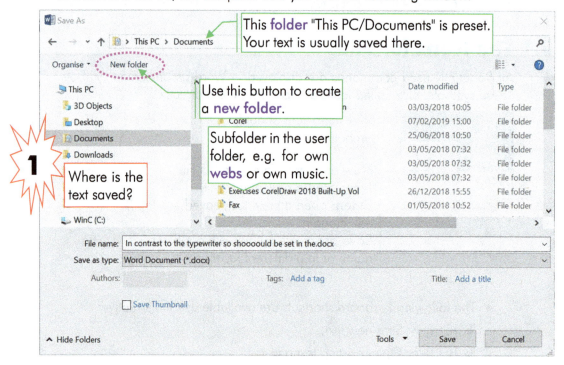

To be able to easily distinguish your exercise texts from other files, you should save them in a subfolder "Exercises Word 2016 - first volume". In a computer course, it is, of course, recommended to use the course number as the folder name.

> Press "New Folder":

The new folder is already selected and can be over-written immediately with "Exercises Word 2016 - First Volume", then confirm with Return.

> The new folder can now be opened by double-clicking on it and
> enter the desired name for this file in the menu below, we want to save this text as "error text".

3.3 Folder, File Name, and File Extension

◆ A saved text is stored as a **file** on a data carrier (hard disk, USB stick, etc.).

  ✎ The files on your hard disk will also be used if you later create a calculation or a computer image.

◆ Each file is given a **file name** and a **file extension** is appended as well as a **docx** for Word documents, the abbreviation for a document.

  ✎ For example, Internet pages are given the file extension htm for HTML for differentiation purposes.

> The file name can be up to 255 characters long from Windows 95. Spaces are also allowed but not the following special characters: / \ < > * ? " " | : ;
> It works, but it is better not to use a dot because the file extension starts after a dot!

Make the file extension visible:

Here is a short guide: in **Windows Explorer** Organize/Folders and Search **Options**, remove the tick at "Hide extensions for known file types" on the View tab.

Check every time you first save:

◆ **Where** is the file stored (= in which folder, on which drive)?

◆ **What** Filename?

To the folders:

◆ These files are sorted into **folders** because there are so many files. The only function of the folders is to keep them organized.

  ✎ Just think of traditional file folders. They can also be used to search for and file suitable documents.

  ✎ For example, if all letters are sorted in a folder **C:\Texts\Letters**, you can find them at any time and

  ✎ You do not need to specify "Letter" in every file name (instead *of "Letter to Walter Example" you only need to specify "Walter Example" in the Letters folder*).

Notes: ....

          ....

          ....

          ....

          ....

          ....

3.4 End Text or Word

The ⊠ (X of Exit) on the top right close's documents and programs:

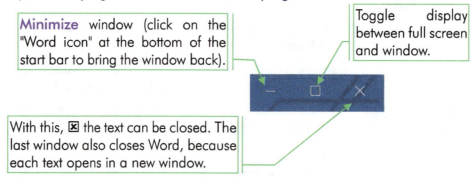

Minimize window (click on the "Word icon" at the bottom of the start bar to bring the window back).

Toggle display between full screen and window.

With this, ⊠ the text can be closed. The last window also closes Word, because each text opens in a new window.

♦ Alternatively, you can also "close" a text in the **File** menu.

   ↳ A question menu appears if a text or its last changes has not yet been saved.

➢ Use one of these methods to **close** the text.

♦ **Minimize** or **Exit**?

   ↳ Minimize means that the program remains active and in the working memory but is not displayed on the screen.

   ↳ It is advisable to **terminate** programs that you no longer need for a longer period of time in order to relieve the working memory!

3.5 About the Save

> Remember to save regularly because your computer occasionally goes out of order and stops responding (in computer language: **crashes**). Ideally, if an action is successful or if you have already written some text.

♦ Note: a question will appear in a text or recent changes have not yet been saved:

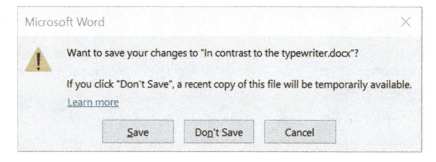

> It is advisable to close all texts that you are no longer working on immediately in order to know whether you want to save a text.

Otherwise, at the end of a working day, you may still have some texts open and need to think carefully about whether you want to save them, or their changes, or risk losing changes you just can't remember.

4. The Font Settings

You are now familiar with Windows and window basics. It's time to start with the essentials, Word-Processing. Of course, we'll start all over again. You can simply continue with the next page if you are already familiar with it.

4.1 The Select

We will learn to change the appearance of the text in this exercise.

- ◆ Adjusting the appearance of a text is called Formatting.

  | Formatting |

  - ↳ For example, you can adjust the following: font type, size, **bold**, *italic*, <u>underlined</u>, color, etc.

Procedure:

- ◆ At this point, not just a letter is edited, but an entire word or paragraph.

  | Font: Select |

  - ↳ Consequently, the computer needs to know which word or phrase you want to modify.
  - ↳ For this reason, the text passage to be changed must first be selected. Only then can the font setting be varied.

4.1.1 Selecting Goes Like This

- ◆ Double-click a word with the mouse.
- ◆ Click an entire paragraph three times quickly.
- ◆ Press the left mouse button in the left margin of the page to create a whole line.

  | Click here. |

- ◆ Press and hold the [Shift] key, then press the [Directional Keys] or [Page up] / [Page down].
  - ↳ Do not release the [Shift] key until the selection fits!
  - ↳ Select the [Directional Keys] or [Page up] / [Page down] button in the other direction to decrease the selection.
- ◆ Longer Paragraphs with the Mouse: keep the left mouse button pressed, then drag the mouse over the position to be selected.

4.1.2 Select Exercise

Start a new Text again. Write the following text:

> I went to the supermarket empty-handed for grocery shopping.

Use this box to indicate texts that you want to write.

A word can be selected by double-clicking on it. A very good addition is the following.

♦ A selected word can be dragged to another position with the mouse:
  - Hold the mouse down, move away and note the pseudo-cursor that indicates the destination.
  - Do not release the mouse until the correct position has been selected.

➢ Repeat the above sentence as follows:

> I went to the supermarket for shopping - without money!

More to try out:

➢ Click three times to select the entire sentence (= select paragraph),

➢ click again, so that the selection disappears, then

➢ select the sentence by clicking in the margin to the left side.

Note that Word automatically sets the space bar correctly!

4.2 Change Font

Write the next Text, then format as specified.

> normal, **bold**, *italic*, underlined, blue highlighted

The three options available are:

♦ select either the font drop-down list or an icon at startup: e.g., **B** for Bold

♦ or press the right mouse button on the highlighted area, then click on Font in the drop-down menu or use the displayed toolbar.

Use the icons on the left to format the image. The highlighting **B** *I* <u>U</u> ▾ will be explained on the next page. All you need to do is click on a word and select several words.

4.3 Highlight Color

In Word, there is a symbol with the effect of a wide **Felt-marker**. You can use it to mark text passages in color, which is also printed on a color printer:

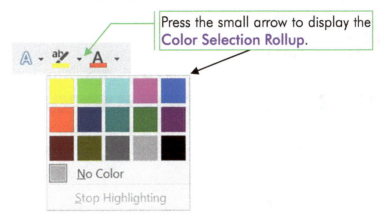

Press the small arrow to display the **Color Selection Rollup**.

No Color

Stop Highlighting

Procedure:

♦ Either **select first**, then press the felt marker icon or the color selection arrow.

↳ The selection is painted in the selected color.

↳ Use the arrow to select a different color.

♦ Or click on the **felt marker** icon or on a color from the **color selection rollup**. Now the felt marker is visibly switched on and you can highlight any part of the text:

↳ Targeting with a pressed mouse, e.g., only the first letter or several words or

↳ a highlighted Word with a double click or a paragraph with three clicks, etc.

↳ Press the Felt-Marker icon again to end the function.

♦ **Remove** Highlighting:

↳ Select, then select color selection arrow and choose "**No Color**" instead of color or

↳ the first color "**None**", then paint highlighted areas.

One more Practice:

➢ **Select** the entire line by clicking once on the left and press [Ctrl] - [Spacebar].

↳ All settings are now reset, except the highlighting. Remove them as described above.

➢ Reset everything using the **right MOUSE BUTTON/FONT**.

> All setting options are summarized in the **Font** menu. There you can search for rarely used formatting, e.g., double underlined, otherwise use the practical symbols.

[Ctrl]-[Space] resets font settings.

4.4 Change Font Size

Icons are not only available for bold and italic. The font and its size can also be set quickly using the following buttons.

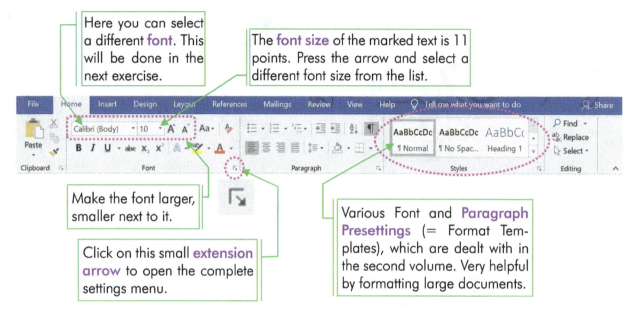

Here you can select a different font. This will be done in the next exercise.

The font size of the marked text is 11 points. Press the arrow and select a different font size from the list.

Make the font larger, smaller next to it.

Click on this small extension arrow to open the complete settings menu.

Various Font and Paragraph Presettings (= Format Templates), which are dealt with in the second volume. Very helpful by formatting large documents.

Start a new Exercise:

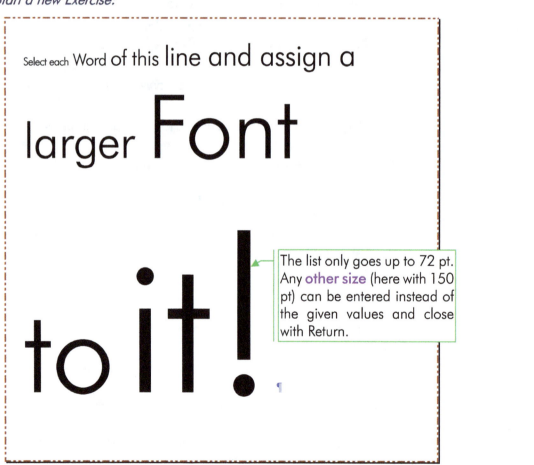

Select each Word of this line and assign a

larger Font

to it!

The list only goes up to 72 pt. Any other size (here with 150 pt) can be entered instead of the given values and close with Return.

➢ Once done, save as "font size" and as our practice folder.

4.5 Set Font

There are generally two ways to change the font:

◆ either via the button in the **toolbar**:

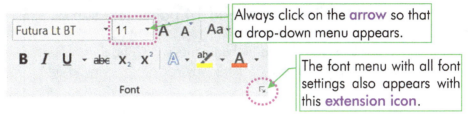

Always click on the **arrow** so that a drop-down menu appears.

The font menu with all font settings also appears with this **extension icon**.

◆ or in the **Font menu**:

↳ Select text, **right mouse button** on the selection, then select **font**. A menu with the important font settings also appears with the right mouse button.

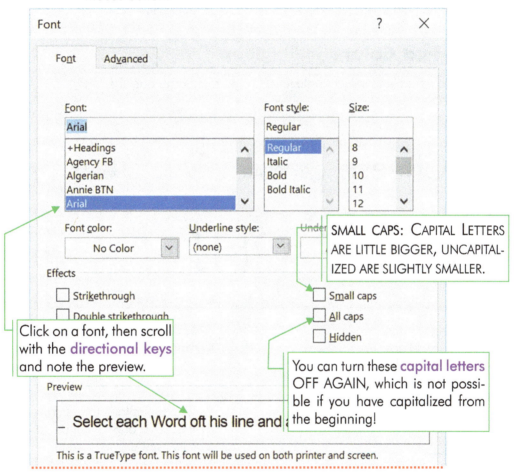

Click on a font, then scroll with the **directional keys** and note the preview.

SMALL CAPS: CAPITAL LETTERS ARE LITTLE BIGGER, UNCAPITAL-IZED ARE SLIGHTLY SMALLER.

You can turn these **capital letters** OFF AGAIN, which is not possible if you have capitalized from the beginning!

➢ **Write** the following exercise text and change the font approximately as shown, then save as "Exercise Font":

Every Word, **every letter,** *letter, a different* FONT.¶

Other Font with 20 pt.

Now try this Exercise:

➤ First, write the Text, then format it as shown here (first select the area or Word, then format).

Please set this line to bold and 14 points font size. ¶

And in this line, you should highlight the word "underline". The font menu can be double, dotted, wavy or double waved underlined. ¶

It is sometimes better to highlight a word in *italics* instead of underlining or **bold**. ¶

➤ When done, save the following exercise as "Underline" and "Text Color".

4.6 The Text Color

It is also possible to select single letters, e.g., to enlarge only the O's:

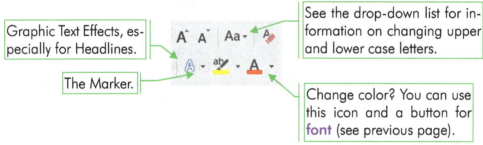

Graphic Text Effects, especially for Headlines.

The Marker.

See the drop-down list for information on changing upper and lower case letters.

Change color? You can use this icon and a button for font (see previous page).

Help for Selecting:

♦ Single letters are often difficult to mark with the mouse. The following is more practical for targeted marking:

↳ Move the cursor with the directional keys in front or behind the letters, then hold down the **[Shift] key**.

↳ While pressing the [Shift] key, you can use the directional keys to highlight or the

↳ directional key in the other direction reduces the marking.

5. Paragraph Settings

5.1 Basic Principles

Paragraph:
Mark unnec-
essarily

- ◆ If you change the character formatting (font, font size, etc.), you must first select what you want to change. ¶

- ◆ The paragraph settings are different: Line spacing, space before or after, paragraph orientation (left, right, centered, justification), etc. ¶

  - ↳ These settings automatically apply to the entire paragraph.

  - ↳ A new paragraph should begin with each return. ¶

- ◆ Therefore, paragraphs do not have to be selected. ¶

  - ↳ All you have to do is place the cursor in the paragraph by clicking anywhere in the paragraph. ¶

  - ↳ Move the mouse away so that you do not confuse the mouse arrow with the cursor. ¶

- ◆ Therefore, there is a second option besides the paragraph mark (Return): use [Shift]-Return (=new line) to force a new line, but remain in the same paragraph with the same settings. ¶

> Paragraphs consist of several lines. Each text should be structured into clearly recognizable paragraphs. This makes it easier for the reader to grasp the context by pausing for thought after reading a paragraph.

- ◆ However, in many cases paragraphs are created by pressing Return twice.

  - ↳ This is not an optimal method because the paragraph spacing caused by empty paragraphs cannot be adjusted.

As an illustration of two paragraphs with adjusted distance:

This is a sample text. This is a sample text. This is a sample text. This is a sample text. This is a sample text. This is a sample text. This is a sample text. This is a sample text.¶

The Paragraph
Spacing.

This is a sample text. This is a sample text. This is a sample text. This is a sample text. This is a sample text. ¶

5.2 Display Paragraph Marks

Each **paragraph** ends with a paragraph marker. The difference between a new paragraph and a new line is extremely important later in the Progress Volume, but working with a text is already made easier when we see the paragraph marks. ¶

> Paragraph marks or line breaks are so-called **formatting characters**, i.e., characters that are displayed on the screen and saved in the file but are not printed.

To make orientation easier for you, the **paragraph marks** (¶) and **line breaks** (↵) are printed alongside these and the following pages.

Paragraph mark

The display can be activated in two ways: ¶

♦ This icon turns all **formatting characters** on or off.

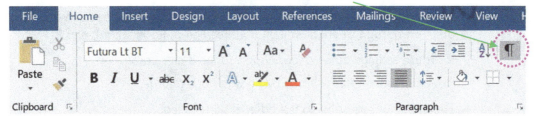

However, you can only show or hide all formatting characters with this **Icon**. Use the following procedure to select what you want to see on the screen:

➢ Click on "**Options**" in the drop-down list of the **file**, then select "**Display**" on the left.

➢ Attempt to display the paragraph marks and spaces at that point.

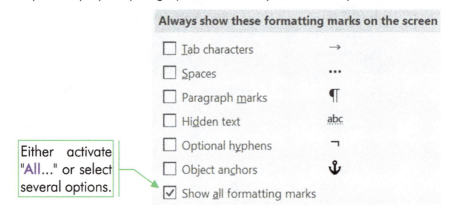

*Either activate "**All**..." or select several options.*

Word Settings:

♦ All Word settings are grouped together in **File/Options**.

✎ In the menu item **Display**, you can switch the display of some elements on or off.

✎ Under **Advanced** you will find a long list with all further setting options of Word.

Paragraph marks switched on? Then try the following exercise:

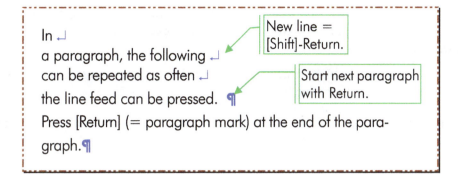

Explanation:

> A **Paragraph** is a coherent Text Block.
>
> It is recommended that you have **Return** set the line breaks only at the end of the paragraph, otherwise Word set the line breaks, and only press **[Shift]-Return** for a new line within the paragraph if required, so that you can set a **spacing** or this paragraph completely flush left or right before and after this paragraph.

5.3 Alignment

Those were the essential basics. Now paragraphs are being edited. And the most important thing is the alignment of the paragraph, where you should again use the **Icons** (instead of the **Paragraph** menu) because this is the faster way:

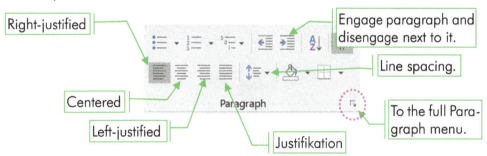

New Exercise:

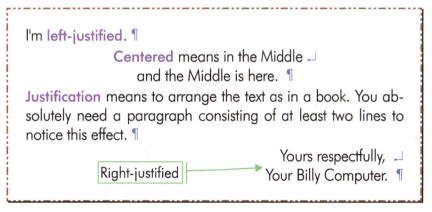

5.4 The Paragraph Settings

You can set the paragraph and line spacing exactly in the paragraph menu, which you can access in several ways after you have placed the cursor in the paragraph:

♦ **Right mouse button/paragraph** or press the icon, the **small expansion arrow** (large Fig. Previous page):   Paragraph   ⌐ₓ

Instead of setting endless blank lines, the distance between the **paragraphs** can be determined here and advantageous to conversely be adjusted at any time.

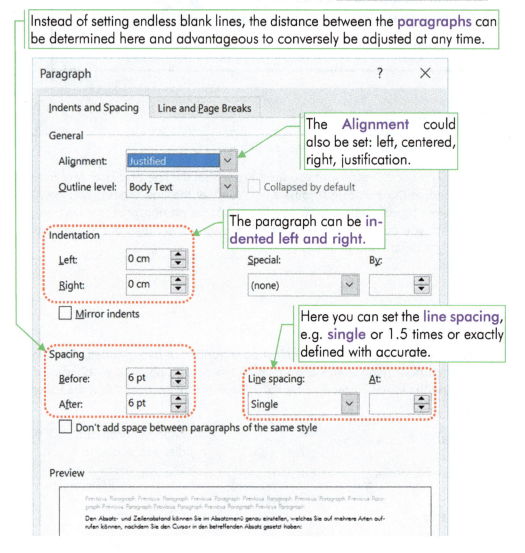

The **Alignment** could also be set: left, centered, right, justification.

The paragraph can be in-dented left and right.

Here you can set the **line spacing**, e.g. **single** or 1.5 times or exactly defined with accurate.

As an illustration:

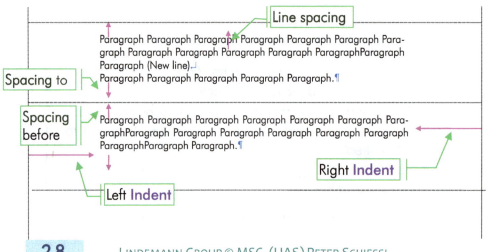

5.4.1 Exercise on the Paragraph Settings

First, write and Indent as indicated in the text:

> I'm **Justification** and left and right indented *by 2 inches.* ¶

You can now format the above paragraph to **1.5 lines spacing**:

> I'm **Justification** and left and
>
> right indented *by 4 inches.* ¶

And now select **Precisely** with *15 points* line spacing:

> I am **right justified** and addi-
> tionally left around 3, right
> around 0.5 *inches* indented. ¶

5.5 Undo

Nothing more can happen to you with the following:

- ♦ Note the result on the **screen** for each action.
- ♦ If the expected has not occurred, select **Undo** immediately.
  - ↳ Find the cause (wrong command, unchecked, etc.) and find the correct command.

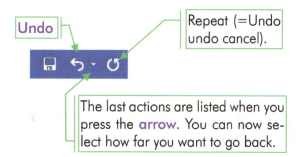

Undo

Repeat (=Undo undo cancel).

The last actions are listed when you press the **arrow**. You can now select how far you want to go back.

Note: **Repeat** = **Restore** only works if something has been undone before.

5.6 Font and Paragraph Exercise

Seminar

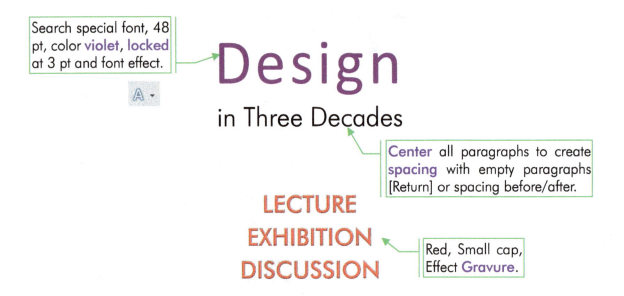

Search special font, 48 pt, color **violet**, **locked** at 3 pt and font effect.

Design

in Three Decades

Center all paragraphs to create **spacing** with empty paragraphs [Return] or spacing before/after.

LECTURE
EXHIBITION
DISCUSSION

Red, Small cap, Effect **Gravure**.

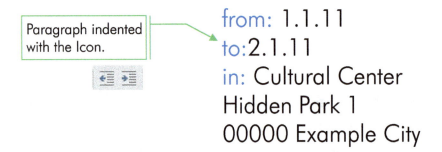

Paragraph indented with the Icon.

from: 1.1.11
to: 2.1.11
in: Cultural Center
Hidden Park 1
00000 Example City

Small Instructions:

All the necessary settings for the **font** or **paragraph** can be found except for the last point.

➢ Write the text, then select all paragraphs and **center** them.

➢ The **spacing** can still be created by empty paragraphs with [Return] or by setting a paragraph spacing.

➢ Click paragraph by paragraph now and set it similar to the illustration.

➢ A-Frame around the whole Page? Select **Frame** and **Shading** for this icon arrow and select an effect on the Margin tab.

6. The Word Structure

In the following section, you will get to know the essential elements of the program structure.

6.1 The Program Window

The **menu volume**. For each generic term you will find suitable commands, e.g. most needed at startup, page layout, page settings, etc.

Exit with the **X** or reduce the window with the " ▬ ".

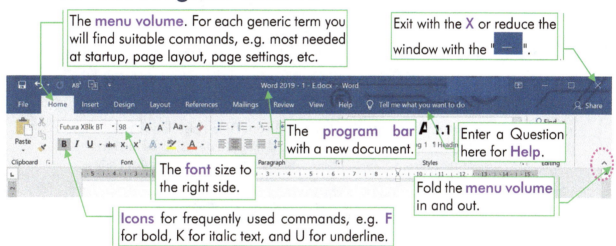

The **program bar** with a new document.

Enter a Question here for **Help**.

The **font** size to the right side.

Fold the **menu volume** in and out.

Icons for frequently used commands, e.g. **F** for bold, K for italic text, and U for underline.

The variety of options is quite confusing in the beginning. That is why the structure will now be explained step by step.

6.2 The Status Line

At the bottom of Word is the status bar, which sometimes displays useful information; the associated menu opens when you click an item:

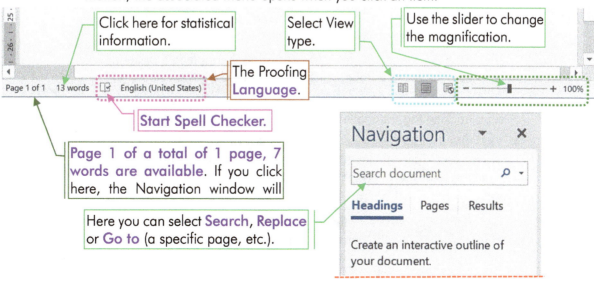

Click here for statistical information.

Select View type.

Use the slider to change the magnification.

The Proofing **Language**.

Start Spell Checker.

Page 1 of a total of 1 page, 7 words are available. If you click here, the Navigation window will

Here you can select **Search**, **Replace** or **Go to** (a specific page, etc.).

Navigation

Search document

Headings Pages Results

Create an interactive outline of your document.

6.3 Menus and Windows

There is space for marked icons in the wide menu volume, which is especially helpful for beginners.

- ♦ At the top of the Quick Access Toolbar, there are basic commands like minimizing Window or Save and Undo. More icons can be added to the arrow:

- ♦ With File, you can save, open, close, print, and so on.

- ♦ At Start, a selection of the most frequently used commands is displayed: Paste (previously copied), essential font and paragraph settings, ready-made font settings for selection, and format templates (explained in the second volume).

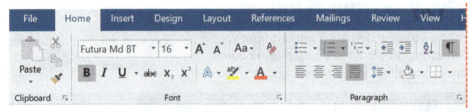

- ♦ With Insert, you can insert anything you want: Title page, page break, table, graphic, clip art, shapes, diagram, hyperlinks, cross-references or headers, footers, page numbers and quick links (formerly AutoText), to name a few.

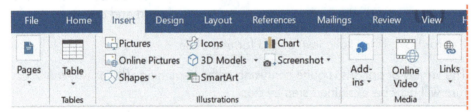

- ♦ Design: various Design suggestions.

- ♦ Layout: Paper format, Page margins, Columns, Prefabricated Designs (color samples) etc.

- ♦ References is a point for advanced users: Table of contents, Footnotes, Quote from another text, Captions, etc.

- ♦ Mailings: All commands for serial printing (serial letters or serial envelopes or labels in serial printing) can be found for Mailings.

- ♦ Review lets you start the spell checker, translate text, add a comment, set a tracking tag, or enable the Track Changes feature.

- ♦ View: All the functions that affect the display on the screen are sorted in when View, such as the display type, ruler, zoom and the window functions and oddly enough the macros.

Depending on the size of the Word window, only icons or, if there is more space, icons with names or only headings are displayed.

6.4 Dialog Boxes

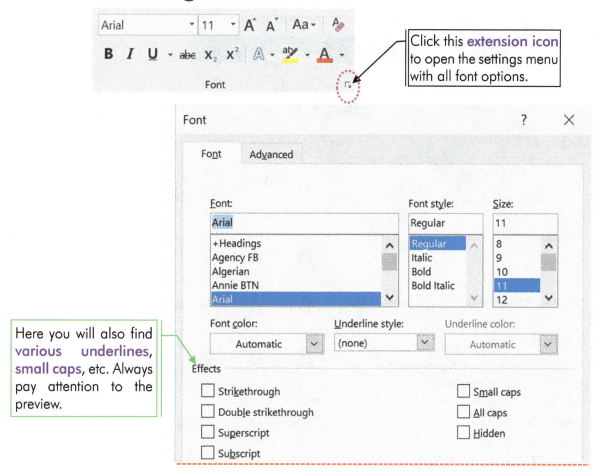

Click this **extension icon** to open the settings menu with all font options.

Here you will also find **various underlines**, **small caps**, etc. Always pay attention to the preview.

6.5 Mouse Clicks

The **cursor** is the blinking line on the screen that indicates the current position in the text. You can move the cursor using the direction keys or the mouse. Do not confuse the cursor with the **mouse arrow**.

Basic information about Mouse operation:

♦ The **left mouse button** is almost always clicked **once:** Select, move Cursor, click Icon.

♦ **Double click** with the left mouse button marks whole words, opens or starts. Except for icons, click once to start.

♦ **Keep left mouse button pressed** to **move** previously selected segments or to select areas as well as text areas.

♦ With the **right mouse button**, selected commands appear for the segment on which you press the key (context-sensitive menu).

  ↳ The right mouse button is, therefore, an **abbreviation** of standard commands.

Frequently try the **right mouse button** which usually displays the appropriate commands.

♦ Some mice still have a **wheel**. You can scroll through long texts by turning the wheel.

6.6 Selection Buttons

If you press the arrow next to a button, a drop-down list open.

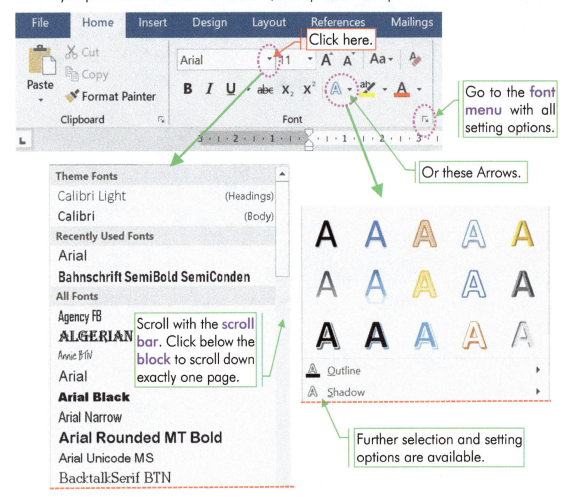

6.7 Final Overview

♦ At the top is the program bar. In addition to Microsoft Word, the name of the current text is also displayed here. If it says "Document 1 (2, 3 ...) - Microsoft Word", it means that the text has not yet been saved!

♦ Then follows the ribbon file-startup-insert draft...

   ✎ For example, press View. All commands are combined there to set the screen display.

♦ Then finally the text window. Our sheet of paper to write on. Preferably stick to the view print layout, and you'll see the page as it would be printed.

♦ The scroll bars are located on the right and bottom of the text window.

   ✎ If the text is too long and no longer fits on the screen, you can scroll through it using the scroll bars. Or with the image up/down on the keyboard.

♦ At the bottom of the status line, the page number is displayed and the view type and magnification can be selected.

➢ The menus can be opened by clicking on these segments, s. page 31.

7. View and Templates

7.1 Shopping List Exercise

The following is a simple exercise to become familiar with Word, to try saving and to set up some text.

Write a simple shopping list (new document):

The font and font size can be selected from the toolbar:

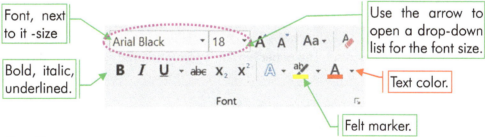

7.1.1 Set Text

To let MS Word recognize which word you want to change, first highlight it, then set it.

> Now mark all further lines with the pressed mouse button and choose another font, size, and color.

> Activate a bulleted character with the minus icon, all paragraphs from bread to salad should be marked for this.

> Save as "shopping list" in the exercise folder.

7.2 Zoom and View Type

There is information about the page number on the left at the bottom and practical icons on the right to select the type of display and enlarge or reduce the view.

Adjust the View:

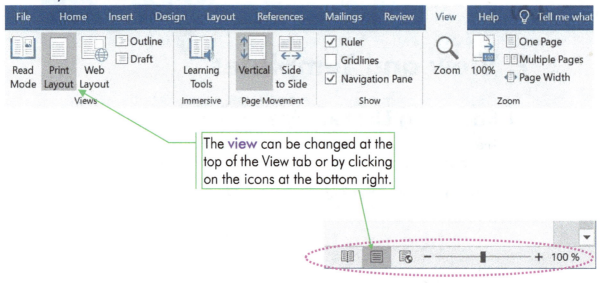

You can switch here:

♦ The best variant is the **print layout** (page layout) for display as printed.

♦ **Read mode** (back with [Esc]): Area of text is extended and icons are hidden, therefore, they are only conditionally suitable for editing.

♦ **Web layout** for Web page Display and Creation

♦ **Outline view**: the table of contents is displayed on the left and is useful for orientation with extensive texts.

♦ **Design** for pure text display without formatting.

> The optimal view is **"Print Layout"**, where you see your document as it would be printed. The paper border is also displayed so that a text can be perfectly designed.

7.3 Other Similar Texts

Once you have written and saved a text, you can open it again at any time to edit the text again or use it as a template for another similar text, because it is best to save it under a new name with **File-"Save as"** so that you do not accidentally overwrite the template letter with the new letter.

♦ If you press **File**, then **New**, you have a new, empty document.

　🖑 Note the selection window in which you can also select a **template**.

　🖑 Numerous **other templates** can be downloaded **online** (enter a search term at the top of **Search for online templates**).

7.4 CD Insert Exercise

➢ Start a new, empty document with File-New and write a CD insert:

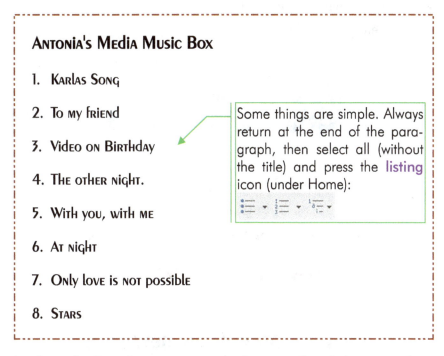

ANTONIA'S MEDIA MUSIC BOX

1. KARLAS SONG

2. TO MY FRIEND

3. VIDEO ON BIRTHDAY

4. THE OTHER NIGHT.

5. WITH YOU, WITH ME

6. AT NIGHT

7. ONLY LOVE IS NOT POSSIBLE

8. STARS

Some things are simple. Always return at the end of the paragraph, then select all (without the title) and press the listing icon (under Home):

➢ Open the Page Setup menu on the Layout tab with the expansion arrow and set the paper dimensions Height 118 mm and Width 151 mm and the page margins on the Paper tab to 1.5 cm throughout.

➢ Format text appropriately and save it to your exercise folder.

7.4.1 Save File as

The command "Save as" is a simple method when you want to make a copy. Then you can select a different folder or drive (e.g., the floppy drive) or assign a different file name (e.g., copy of .... am).

➢ Save as "Antonia Media Music Box", then create a copy with File-Save as and overwrite the texts for another CD insert.

➢ Try to print this sheet with File-Printing, maybe it will work, otherwise, a more detailed instruction will follow later.

7.5 Template Exercise

Using ready-made templates is not difficult at all.

➢ Start a letter using a letter template: File, then New and then select a letter template and overwrite the default text.

➢ Save in a new folder "Letters" as "Letter to XY Date".

Also, in this case, you could save the next letter under a new name with File-Save and then only change the text appropriately, so all settings and formatting are taken over.

7.6 Stroller Exercise

A little exercise for font adjustment.

➢ Start a new file, write and set text,

➢ and then save it as "Stroller display".

Strollers

for sale!!!

Modell Sport Wagon Turbo XXL
Super Speed 3 Plus E Comfort

TÜV and CE tested, approved up to 8 km/h

Almost like new, only used for three years

included for half the new price

Description and accessories!

Phone.: 45 56 67 – FAX: 45 56 68–Email: my@myemail.uk

7.7 Summary

You should now be able to do the following:

♦ Font and paragraph settings such as font type, color, paragraph spacing, alignment, and indentation.

♦ Save as: Here you can specify the name of the file and the storage location (drive, folder) again when saving, also good to use a text as a template for the next similar text.

♦ Start a new text or save and close a new text, based on a template, as well as texts sorted into folders.

Start a new text or save and close a new text, based on a template, as well as texts sorted into folders.

8. Multiple Texts/Windows

Try it out:

> ➤ Close all texts, then with **File/Open**, then reopen both the shopping list and the CD insert.
>
> > ↳ In Word, under **File/Open**, you will find the **most recently edited texts**; you can use the Search command to open additional texts.
>
> ➤ **Open** two additional empty texts with **File/New/Empty** Document and the calculator with **Start/Calculator**.
>
> > ↳ Each new text first gets a name **Document 1, 2, 3 …**
> >
> > ↳ This will tell you if a text has already been saved!

Now we've opened up enough to practice switching:

Here you can see all **open documents** and change them.

1 Shopping list.docx
2 Antonias Media
3 Document3
4 Document4

Try both methods to switch between texts or programs:

> ➤ **Switch** to the other text by clicking on it in **View/Switch Windows**.
>
> ➤ With **[Alt]-[Tab]**, you can also switch to the calculator:
> Hold down [Alt], then [Tab], briefly click the Tab key.

Note that the **calculator** is not displayed in Word - only text is displayed in Word.

Via the Windows Start Bar:

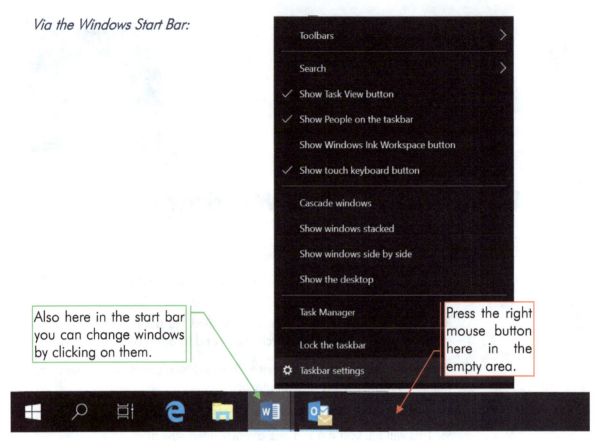

Also here in the start bar you can change windows by clicking on them.

Press the right mouse button here in the empty area.

Every Windows computer can look different. Browse your computer to see if you can start Word faster.

8.1.1 Adjust Window Size

Now you can quit a program or send it to the background. For each **program window**, you can **set the exact size** and move the window.

♦ You can move the window by holding down the left mouse button at the top of the colored bar.

♦ If you have not set the full-screen view: move the mouse slowly over the window border. The mouse arrow changes to a **double arrow**. Now keep the left mouse button pressed and you can set the window size.

   ✍ You can change the **window width** at the left and right edges,

   ✍ the **height** at the top and bottom of the window and the

   ✍ **Window corners** in both dimensions at the same time.

♦ **Switch window** with **[Alt]-[Tab]**: Hold down [Alt] and click [Tab] until the desired window is selected.

   ✍ You can jump back and forth not only between open texts but also between different started programs in this way, e.g., to copy an address from a telephone directory into a Word letter.

   ✍ For this reason, it is very useful for you if you are well versed in window technology.

   ➢ **Try out these options on the exercise texts.**

[Alt]–
[Tab]

8.2 Birthday Invitation with Page Frame

Sometimes, when we see the sheet of paper in the background, we want to look at the whole page to check the layout, but for editing, we want to see the text as large as possible.

➢ Start a new text, **set DIN A5 for layout/format** and landscape format (=size width 21, height 15cm) for alignment and write this for example:

> Birthday Invitation!
>
> I hereby invite you officially and cordially to my birthday on 33.3. of this year. Please bring many gifts and good mood.

➢ Choose a large, bold font for the **headline** and good-looking **hand-writing** with the right font size for **the text**, so that the sheet is filled nicely.

With the zoom slider:

♦ Either adjust the magnification with the slider or click on the +/- button:

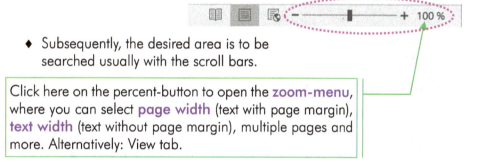

♦ Subsequently, the desired area is to be searched usually with the scroll bars.

Click here on the percent-button to open the **zoom-menu**, where you can select **page width** (text with page margin), **text width** (text without page margin), multiple pages and more. Alternatively: View tab.

A frame around the entire page can be perfectly set up in the Print Layout view:

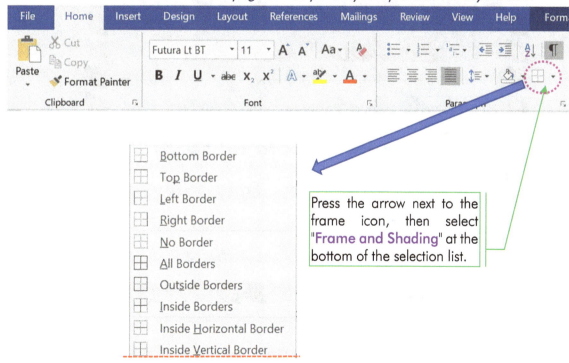

Press the arrow next to the frame icon, then select "**Frame and Shading**" at the bottom of the selection list.

They can be adjusted nicely in the <u>Borders and Shading</u> menu:

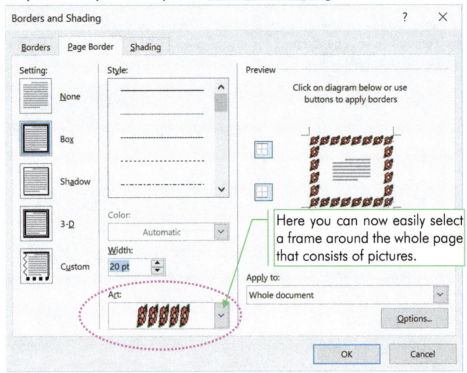

> ➢ If the frame is present, format the text accordingly so that the sheet is filled.

> ➢ Then save the text as a "**Birthday Invitation**".

> ➢ Then switch between the views.

You can see the sheet as it would be printed in the Page Layout view:

8.3 The Scroll Bar

In a book, you can turn the pages. In a computer program, you can scroll using the [Page up/down] buttons or the scroll bars.

> ➤ Open the birthday text, enlarge the text and resize the window until the scroll bars appear and navigate through the scroll bar options.

The Function of the Scroll Bar:

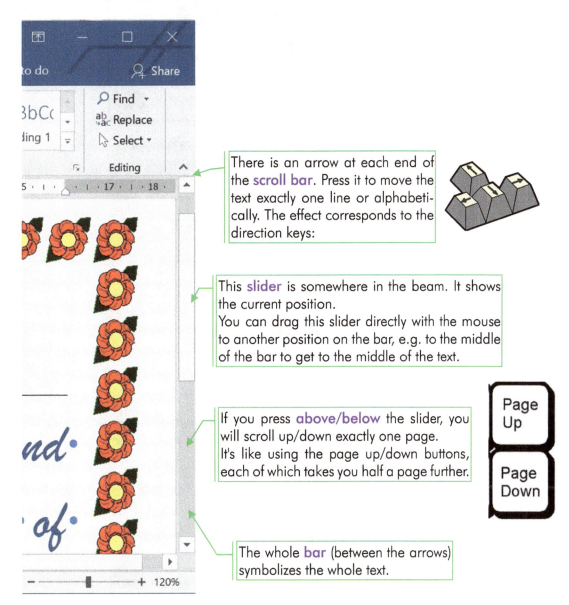

There is an arrow at each end of the scroll bar. Press it to move the text exactly one line or alphabetically. The effect corresponds to the direction keys:

This slider is somewhere in the beam. It shows the current position.
You can drag this slider directly with the mouse to another position on the bar, e.g. to the middle of the bar to get to the middle of the text.

If you press above/below the slider, you will scroll up/down exactly one page.
It's like using the page up/down buttons, each of which takes you half a page further.

The whole bar (between the arrows) symbolizes the whole text.

Enlarge the view considerably so that you can perform this exercise:

> ➤ Move all the way down by pulling the slider all the way down. Always note the slider. Move up again by pressing in the scroll bar above the slider.

> ➤ Now move to the left and right using the horizontal scroll bar. The horizontal scroll bar is only displayed if the entire text is not visible. Try this by experimenting with the zoom slider at the bottom right.

8.4 Scroll Bar and Copy Exercise

Let's write a little book, so start a new text.

➢ Write "My First Book" as the title,

➢ then write a paragraph e.g., with this philosophical text after Return:

> My First Book
>
> This is an exercise text. An exercise text for handling word processing. A pure exercise texts. Nothing more than an exercise text. A boring exercise text, which should not distract from the actual goal of learning word processing. This is my exercise text. A text without mistakes.

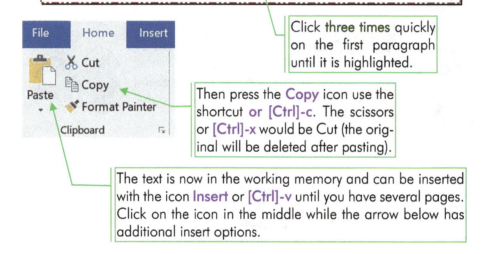

Click **three times** quickly on the first paragraph until it is highlighted.

Then press the **Copy** icon use the shortcut **or [Ctrl]-c**. The scissors or **[Ctrl]-x** would be Cut (the original will be deleted after pasting).

The text is now in the working memory and can be inserted with the icon **Insert** or **[Ctrl]-v** until you have several pages. Click on the icon in the middle while the arrow below has additional insert options.

➢ Note the page number at the bottom left of the status bar.

> When you paste a paragraph for the first time, it is overwritten because the paragraph you copied is still selected. This is not a problem now; however, the selection must be deactivated later by moving the cursor.

➢ You can drag the **block** in the scroll bar with the mouse to move it to the center if you have **multiple pages**.

  ✎ Note that when you move the block, the page on which you would be if you let go of the block is displayed.

> Typical Inherent Error: You must remain in the scroll bar track when dragging the block.

➢ Move the **slider** to the end of the text. Now press above the slider in the scroll bar. Scroll up exactly one page.

➢ You can also scroll with the **image buttons** and, if necessary, with the **wheel** on your mouse, if available.

➢ Move to the end with **[Ctrl]-End** or to the beginning of the text with **[Ctrl]-Pos1**.

➢ **Save** the file as "My first book".

Second Part

Shapes

Font selection, special Paragraphs,
Frames and Shading

Chapter 9

9. Design with Fonts

Word offers numerous functions with which a normal text can be turned into an appealing presentation.

Certainly, you will not have expected some of the effects of a Word Processor.

9.1 A Headline

Not every font is the same.

- ♦ Not Word, but Windows manages the Fonts.
  - ✎ If you install a printer or a new program, you will often also find numerous new Fonts.
  - ✎ These fonts can be used by any program.

- ➢ Start a new text, create some empty paragraph marks with Return and write at the top:

> Title

- ➢ Save as "Formatting Exercise".

There are normal Scripts, bold Fonts for Headlines, Manuscripts and Special Fonts, for example with holes in the text or icons instead of letters.

So, you should first get an overview of the fonts installed on your computer.

- ➢ Scroll through the font list using the scroll bar to get an overview.

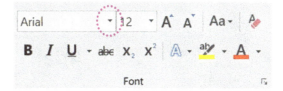

Now we will deal with the various setting options from the icon volume (font list) and the font menu (by an icon or right mouse button to start).

9.2 Font Selection

When selecting fonts, you will find a scroll list with a preview of the fonts:

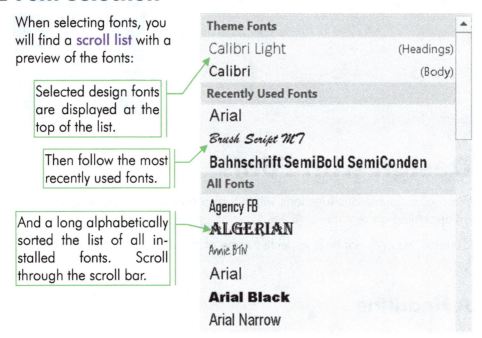

Selected design fonts are displayed at the top of the list.

Then follow the most recently used fonts.

And a long alphabetically sorted the list of all installed fonts. Scroll through the scroll bar.

All setting options are available in the Font menu:

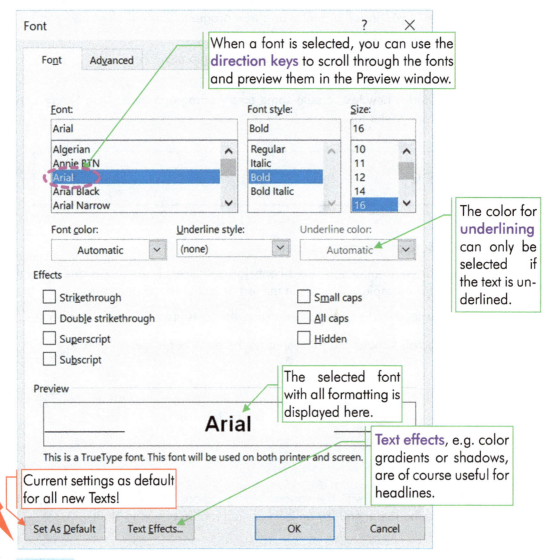

When a font is selected, you can use the direction keys to scroll through the fonts and preview them in the Preview window.

The color for underlining can only be selected if the text is underlined.

The selected font with all formatting is displayed here.

Text effects, e.g. color gradients or shadows, are of course useful for headlines.

Current settings as default for all new Texts!

To the Exercise:

➢ Get an overview of the fonts installed on your computer.

➢ Then choose a thick font for the title text:

Title

9.3 Effects with the Icons

The toolbar also contains some quickly accessible formatting options. Perhaps a bit too much:

Bold, italic, underlined and crossed out: for underlined, further options can be selected with the small arrow (see illustration).

Format currently selected text with a larger or smaller font.

Delete all formatting (settings) for the currently selected text with the default setting.

Use the small arrow to expand the selection list, shown here for text effects, underlining and text color.

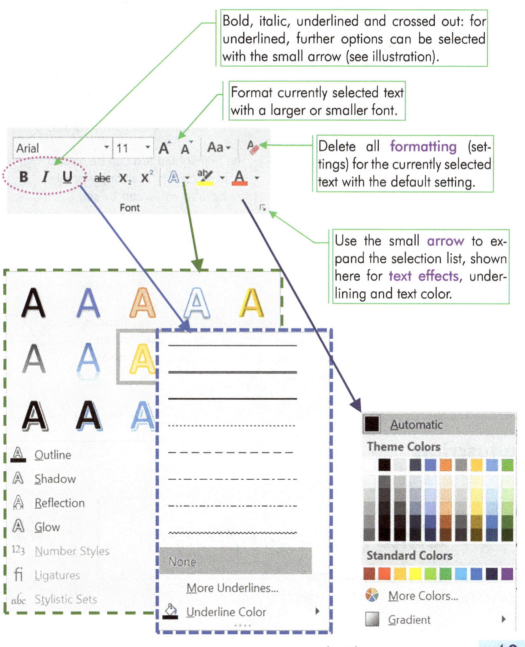

9.4 Lock Font

Now we're going to pull the letters even further apart.

> ➢ Select the right **mouse button** and **font** on the title.
> ➢ **Switch** to the Advanced tab at the top of the menu:

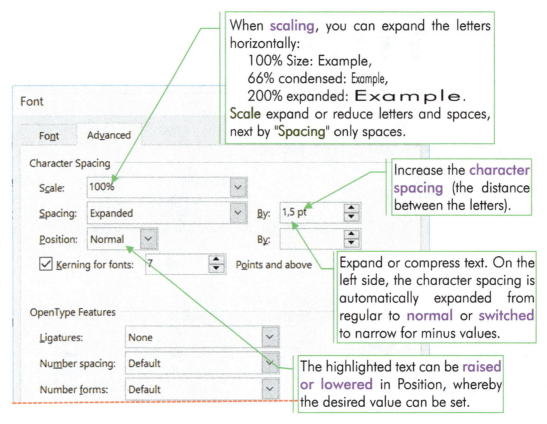

When **scaling**, you can expand the letters horizontally:
  100% Size: Example,
  66% condensed: Example,
  200% expanded: Example.
Scale expand or reduce letters and spaces, next by "**Spacing**" only spaces.

Increase the **character spacing** (the distance between the letters).

Expand or compress text. On the left side, the character spacing is automatically expanded from regular to **normal** or **switched** to narrow for minus values.

The highlighted text can be **raised or lowered** in Position, whereby the desired value can be set.

Text can be l o c k e d
or compressed.

Now the Title is getting nicer:

A text effect was also used here. Besides the default settings below, note the manual setting options for Contours, Shadows, Reflections, and Lights.

9.5 Manuscripts

Change and format the title with a manuscript:

Little Christmas Story

Take your time to explore your Scriptures.

9.6 The Font Manager

♦ Fonts are managed in Windows by the font manager. New fonts, e.g., from a printer or program, are therefore available in every other program under Windows.

♦ You can access the font manager in **Windows** via **Start/Settings/Personalization/Fonts**.

↲ Click on a font to get to the preview menu.

↲ The fonts can be **deleted** in the font manager as follows: click "Uninstall" in the next menu.

↲ To install **new fonts**, use Windows Explorer to find the folder or the drive that contains the font, then right-click the font and choose Install Font.

9.7 Transfer Format

Now that you know a lot about how to format a text, you should also learn how to transfer the settings from one paragraph to another.

The method with the command "**Format Painter**" on the left under Start is also suitable for single words:

Procedure: Click on the correct set text, select the "Transfer format" icon and highlight the new text to be formatted.

There are two alternatives:

♦ Click "**Transfer format**" once for a **one-time** application

♦ or **double-click** to use this function more than once.

↲ Click again on "**Transfer format**" to deactivate.

Transfer Format Exercise:

➤ Write the sentence, then copy it three times as well as **copy** the paragraph three times:

This is an exercise text to transfer the format. This is an exercise text to transfer the format.

This is an exercise text to transfer the format. This is an exercise text to transfer the format. This is an exercise text to transfer the format.

➤ Change the expression "**Format to Transfer**" as follows: Color red, italic, bold, another font.

➤ Select Transfer Format, then click the **Transfer Format** icon once.

↲ Now you have a **brush** on the mouse with which you can paint the next expression of "**Format to transfer**".

➤ Do the same again, but double-click on the "**Transfer format**" icon, then format several new words in the same way. Finally, click on the "Transfer format" icon to turn it off.

9.8 Paragraph Settings Exercise

Write a short poem of your choice and format it, e.g.:

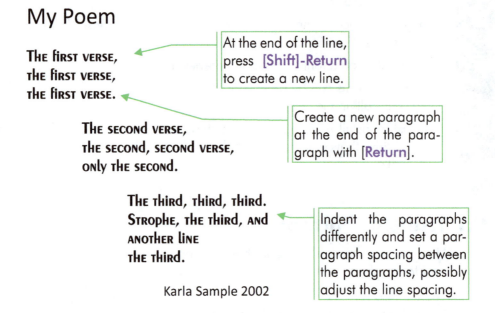

My Poem

The first verse,
the first verse,
the first verse.

At the end of the line, press [Shift]-Return to create a new line.

The second verse,
the second, second verse,
only the second.

Create a new paragraph at the end of the para-graph with [Return].

The third, third, third.
Strophe, the third, and
another line
the third.

Indent the paragraphs differently and set a paragraph spacing between the paragraphs, possibly adjust the line spacing.

Karla Sample 2002

Short instructions:

➢ Do the same again, but double-click on the "Transfer format" icon, then format several new words in the same way. Finally, click on the "Transfer format" icon to turn it off.

➢ Select all text paragraphs and adjust Font as well as Paragraph and Line Spacing.

➢ Finally, try printing the poem with the **File Print** command.

9.9 Indent Paragraphs

Paragraphs can be moved in or out in many ways. A little summary will do.

♦ Use either the **icons** (easiest)

♦ or Indent with the **Tab key**, Indent with the [Back] key, which only works if the cursor is positioned at the beginning or end of the line,

♦ or with the sliders in the **ruler**, as shown on page 54 or in the **right mouse button** paragraph menu (see page 28).

10. Special Paragraphs

After taking a closer look at the font settings, we will now look at how to format the paragraphs more effectively and usefully.

10.1 Hanging Paragraph

A hanging paragraph hangs on the first line. This is very useful for enumerations to increase clarity.

The ideal use cases are lists, e.g., a bibliographical reference or an address list of a club. This is how it should be:

Exercise:

> Müller, Karla: Castle stories. A study of Theodor Fontane's work. Munich 1986 (pp. 96-103). ¶
>
> Müller-Seidel, Walter: Theodor Fontane. Social novel art in Germany. Stuttgart 1975 (pp. 181-196). ¶
>
> Nürnberger, Helmuth: Theodor Fontane, "Cécile". Unknown sketch for a novel. In: Süddeutsche Zeitung, November 11-12, 1978. [1]¶

➢ Write three Paragraphs.

| Important! Return only at the end of the paragraph!

➢ Select all three paragraphs at once by holding down the mouse button in the left margin and dragging from the first to the last paragraph.

➢ Right mouse button over the marker and select paragraph. Or the extension arrow at the paragraph.

---

[1] Quoted and translated into English from: Theodor Fontane: Cécile, DTV-Publishing House, August 1995, ISBN 3-423-02361-9, p. 276-277, printing preparation by Peter Schiessl

10.2 The Paragraph Menu

The menu offers all the settings clearly summarized. Here you can occasionally search for new options.

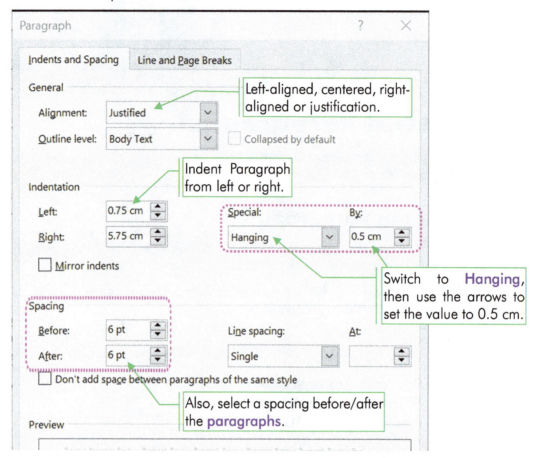

♦ The paragraph spacing can be adjusted as required. The arrows to the right of the button can be used in 6 pt steps, but any desired value can be entered.

This makes the paragraph spacing more advantageous than creating a spacing with empty paragraphs since the latter cannot be adjusted.

Summary:

♦ Press the expansion arrow for font or paragraph or right mouse button on the paragraph and select from the drop-down menu:

♦ Font type for font settings (font type, size, color, etc.),

♦ Paragraph for all paragraph settings (indented, hanging, justification, etc.). Do not highlight, the highlight is only necessary if several paragraphs are to be adjusted at once.

10.3 Hanging with the Ruler

Paragraph indentation can also be adjusted using the ruler.

♦ You can switch the ruler on and off in the View menu.

♦ The ruler can be hidden again after use to get more space for the text.

With the three sliders the paragraph indentation can be made as follows:

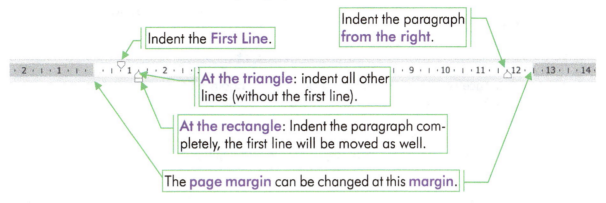

Indent the **First Line**.

Indent the paragraph **from the right**.

At the triangle: indent all other lines (without the first line).

At the rectangle: Indent the paragraph completely, the first line will be moved as well.

The **page margin** can be changed at this **margin**.

> Each change applies only to the **current paragraph**. If you want to change **more than one paragraph**, select all of them first.

➢ Use the **sliders** to change the indentation of the paragraph in the previous exercise, especially the margin.

10.4 Listings

The **hanging paragraph** is also suitable for numbered paragraphs. The numbers are on the outside left while the text is exactly below each other.

Our next topic, a list of questions.

Wishlist for Computer Purchase

1. *Processor, RAM, Hard Disk*? Additional equipment (DVD Burner, WLAN, Bluetooth)? Complete and ready to use?
2. Do not save on RAM! At least 4GB or more!
3. Is the flat screen 22" or better 24" large and faster than 5ms for smooth games and videos?
4. Which *programs* are included, which are needed?
5. How long is the *warranty period*? How long does a *repair* take? Is there telephone support? Does the computer have to be brought into the shop?

The best thing about the *listings* is that Word does them automatically. Follow these steps:

➢ New file, set page format **DIN A5**.

➢ **Write** the text, of course without the numbers at the beginning, while pressing **Return** only at the end of the paragraphs.

➢ Format the **heading**: bold + larger font + italic.

➢ Highlight all paragraphs and set a paragraph spacing of 6 pt before and after each paragraph.

➢ **Select** all four other paragraphs and activate numbering.

This icon is available in the Start menu for numbering:

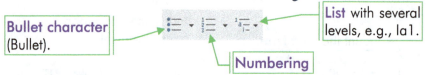

Bullet character (Bullet).

List with several levels, e.g., la1.

Numbering

Clicking once switches the numbering on, clicking again on the icon switches it off again. Switching to another option is also possible. A selection list can be opened with the **mini arrow** next to the Icon.

> Make sure that all the desired paragraphs are highlighted.

The automatic Listing:

- All you have to do is click on the **numbering** icon.
  - All highlighted paragraphs are already marked with numbers.
  - If you add or delete paragraphs, the numbering is automatically **updated**.
  - The settings for the hanging paragraph are also made by Word. You can see this from the sliders of the ruler.

10.4.1 Bullet Character

Alternatively, a bullet can precede a number.

- ➤ **Select** the numbered paragraphs. Then click on the other **bulleted** icon.
  - The small arrow to the right of the icon allows you to expand a selection list:

How to set any bullet character is explained in the second volume of MS Word.

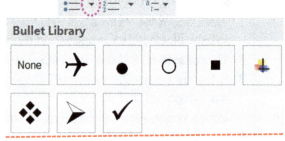

10.5 A Brief Summary

- These were some **paragraph settings** (space before, after, line spacing, indentation, hanging paragraph, listing, and numbering).
  - The hanging paragraph, a numbered or bulleted paragraph, is extremely important later for longer texts: for enumerations, bibliographical references, embroidery points or other lists.
- Are you now aware of the difference between **page**, **paragraph** and **font** formatting?
  - the input via an **icon** (pay attention to scroll menus) or the **right mouse button?**

11. Borders and Shading

11.1 Exercise with Frames

Would you have thought that? In Word, you can not only change the **text color**, e.g., write with blue, but also assign a **frame** to a paragraph.

The **color of the frame** and the **background** are adjustable, e.g., to make the text blue or yellow.

Small Advertisement (please write first again):

Short Tutorial:

> ➢ New exercise, the **paper size** of 12 cm wide and 8 cm high:

>> ✎ Click on "**Size**" for **layout**, then on "**More paper sizes**" and enter the dimensions in the menu above.

> ➢ **Write** the Text.

> ➢ Insert the **dot** as an icon: **Insert** a file card with the icons/More icons.

> ➢ Select all rows and choose **Centered**.

> ➢ Highlight **first line**: Font size 48 Pt, blocked by 15 Pt, bold, red. Alternatively, try a text effect.

11.2 Shading

Let's start with shading, as this is the simpler option.

> ➤ Place the cursor in the text (if you have more than one paragraph with Return, they would have to be selected first), then click on the small triangle so that the scroll menus appear:

Select fill colors, also with shades.

Frames lines and the menu "Frames and shading".

Theme Colors

Standard Colors

No Color

More Colors...

You can underline a paragraph in the Frame drop-down menu with "Borders...", switch off all frames with "No frame" or border a paragraph with "Outside Borders".

Bottom Border
Top Border
Left Border
Right Border
No Border
All Borders
Outside Borders
Inside Borders
Inside Horizontal Border
Inside Vertical Border
Diagonal Down Border
Diagonal Up Border
Horizontal Line
Draw Table
View Gridlines
Borders and Shading...

> ➤ Choose a background color, preferably not too dark, but only slightly shaded.

About the Shading:

♦ On almost all inkjet printers, the strong background color on plain paper causes the color to run out.

    ✍ Better results can be achieved with shallower colors such as the lighter shades of design colors.

♦ The optimum value depends on the type of printer and the type of paper: determine the optimum value with test prints.

Next are the Frame Lines.

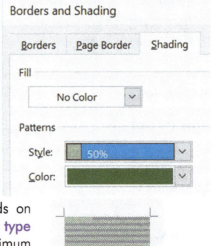

Borders and Shading

Borders	Page Border	Shading

Fill

No Color

Patterns

Style: 50%

Color:

11.3 A Frame Line

The lines appear around a paragraph after shading. You can adjust these at the next icon.

➢ Select "Borders and shading" from the drop-down menu, where we can adjust the desired double line.

➢ Either select a prefabricated setting on the left, e.g., the frame with shadow or

➢ select your own frame lines in the middle with the desired line type, color, and thickness.

➢ With both variants, you can set lines with the mouse or click away on the right side of the preview window and thus, for example, set only one line at the top and bottom instead of a closed box.

Please note the index cards shown on the next page.

In this field, for example, you can set only one line at the top and bottom. Switch the line on or off by clicking on it. The system then automatically switches to Adjust on the left.

The double line is situated further down in the list.

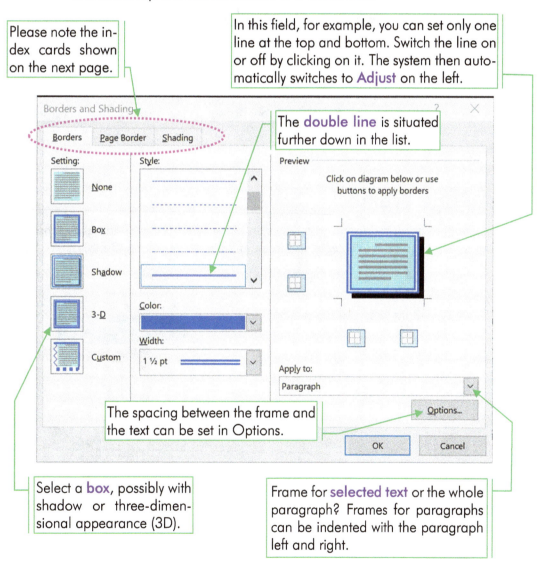

The spacing between the frame and the text can be set in Options.

Select a box, possibly with shadow or three-dimensional appearance (3D).

Frame for selected text or the whole paragraph? Frames for paragraphs can be indented with the paragraph left and right.

The Frames and shading menu also allow you to individually set a shading on the Shading tab or to create a line or special pattern around the entire page on the Margin tab.

11.4 Lines

Tip: A frame can also be used to create a *line* or a bar across the entire text width.

> ➤ Set an **empty paragraph** by Return,

> ➤ then set a *line* for it as shown, either from the drop-down menu or from the Frame and Shading menu. The latter menu offers numerous setting options.

Paragraph with Line:

With filling (pattern on the Shading tab) instead of the line:

◆ Graphic lines can be selected from a list using the "**Horizontal line**" button (Fig. p. 58) at the bottom of the menu.

A horizontal line can also be selected, but not set, in the scroll list of the Frame Lines icon.

11.5 A Page Frame

According to the same principle, you can place a frame (no shading) around the entire page on the "**Effects**" tab in the middle of the "**Margin**" tab.

◆ Note the option to set the **spacing** in the **Options** button

◆ as well as the interesting effect frames with which you can border the page with apples or hearts.

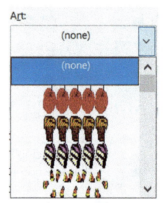

This beautiful and simple alternative was introduced during the "Birthday Invitation" Exercise.

12. Printing

Printing should now be finally mentioned. Select **File Print** or Shortcut **[Ctrl]-P**:

Start **printing** as set below.

Print one or **multiple copies** simultaneously?

You can change the printer here if you have **more than one printer.**

The **Printer Properties dialog** allows you to set your printer, e.g. quick or straight printing.

Select what to print. You can print only the previously marked text with "**Print selection**", e.g. a single sentence.

At the bottom are print options such as single-sided or double-sided, sorted or not, portrait or landscape, margin settings, printing one or more pages and reduced to one sheet.
Such settings are often still available in the printer settings menu.

12.1 Settings

12.1.1 Print Quality and Paper

♦ You can set your printer at the top of Printer Properties. Different settings are available depending on the printer.

    ✎ In most cases, it is possible to switch between quick print with poorer quality, normal print, and best print quality, whereby the latter, of course, requires more time.

    ✎ The option "Print from the last page" is often important, usually to be found on the "Set up page" tab, because printers that print the printed page upwards must print the last page first in order to eject the sheets in the correct order.

> This setting for print quality and paper type is especially important for inkjet printers! You can only achieve good inkjet printouts with the correct paper type setting.

Normal print quality is sufficient when printing on normal paper with an inkjet printer. Photo quality printing is only possible on coated glossy or photo paper, and this can also be set in the menu as the paper/media type with the highest print quality.

12.1.2 What should be Printed

You can print everything or only certain pages.

♦ Current page prints only the page on which the cursor is positioned.

♦ With the Print selection, you can print previously selected text, e.g., only one paragraph from one page. However, this paragraph is then printed at the top edge of the page, not at the original page position.

♦ You can specify specific pages to be printed for pages. You can either separate the page numbers by semicolons or enter a range with a hyphen.
Examples: 3;6;8;9-15;22;29-33

♦ Sorted: this option is important if you print multiple copies, so that Word prints one copy first, then the next instead of five times each page.

♦ Pages per Sheet: Allows you to print multiple pages on the selected paper size, e.g., two pages on one A4 sheet. The pages will be reduced accordingly.

More about printing follows in the second volume, especially what is important for printing documents with multiple pages.

13. More About Saving

As a continuation of Chapter 3, we will now look at saving a bit more thoroughly. It is important to be able to make a copy, e.g., as a data backup or to transport a text on a USB stick.

13.1 Copy File with "Save as"

We can make a copy using the Save As command. This makes this command suitable for another application: if you want to create a similar text, you can open the original and create a copy with "Save as".

Save As stands for Save under a different name or in a different folder or drive. With Save As, you can therefore also make a copy e.g., to a USB stick.

> ➢ Open one of our first exercise texts, e.g., MTB.

> ➢ Connect the USB stick, under select File/Save as and select the USB stick as the destination drive.

> ➢ Add a copy of the date to the file name, specifying the current date instead of the date.

> Attention! Do not continue working on this copy, but close this text and if necessary open the original from the hard disk.

13.2 The Systematics of Saving

♦ First Saving: you are automatically on Save as because you want to specify the folder and file name.

♦ Next Saving: it will be saved to this file without question. The previous version is overwritten!

♦ Save as: an already saved file can also be saved under a different name, in a different folder or on a different drive.

The latter is an important and practical option:

♦ You can make a backup copy by selecting an external storage device as the destination or

♦ the text as a template for a new letter by saving it under a different name and then changing the text accordingly.

13.3 Where, with the Texts?

With time, more and more texts accumulate. To keep the overview, the texts should be stored in folders. We will introduce a simple method to create folders. Further information can be found in our Windows book or in a Windows course.

- ♦ Word 2016 is preset so that your texts are saved in the "Documents" folder (for libraries).
  - ↳ Windows automatically created this folder during installation.
  - ↳ So, you already know where to find your texts.
  - ↳ You should at least create suitable subfolders in this folder.
- ♦ It is even better to create a folder for the texts.
  - ↳ Further subfolders, e.g., letters, reports, logs, circulars, etc. are created in this Texts folder.

If such subfolders are created at an early stage, you will save yourself a lot of time and frustration later on, because you will not find anything in the inevitable data chaos.

> In companies with networked computers, it is best to save all work in a folder with your own name as the folder name in order to tidy up suitable subfolders. This makes it easier for everyone to know who owns these files or where to find them when they are accessed from other computers.

Example of Folder Structure:

Everyone creates different files and needs different folders.

Hard disk C or drive XY:
▪ Folder Adam Smith
o (subfolder) Letters
o (Subfolder) Reports
o (Subfolder) Presentations
o (subfolder) Calculations

13.4 Advantages of Folders

- ♦ You can quickly find the texts and therefore use similar texts as templates.
- ♦ All the Texts can be saved by copying this folder.
- ♦ You can delete texts that are no longer needed because you have an overview and can thus save yourself later clean-up actions or constant frustrations because you do not find texts or have to search for a long time.

Once again, the basic procedure:

- ♦ For example, if you write your first letter, create a subfolder Letters in the Documents folder in exactly the same way.
  - ↳ All other letters are saved in this folder.

> Folders are like real folders to collect and tidy up according to any criterion, e.g., the type (letter, protocol, student research project etc.). With this procedure, you will be able to find your texts easily later.

13.5 Automatic Saving

Unfortunately, almost every computer crashes occasionally. This can be very annoying if you've just finished a nice paragraph or formatted a table nicely and haven't thought about saving it yet.

Word has an automatic memory function to limit the damage. Word cannot save all the time because the computer would then be too busy, but by default, the current status is saved every 10 minutes.

- ♦ You could change the default setting in **File**, then **Options**, by left-clicking **Save**.
  - ✋ Here you can set the time for the automatic backup (AutoRestore…) or switch it off, as well as view in which folder this is saved.

13.6 Restoration

If the computer crashed while a text was open, the Document Recovery window will appear the next time you start MS Word.

You can then select whether you want to continue working with the automatically last saved text or the original text (which you last saved by clicking Save).

The last changes will be lost because MS Word saves only every 10 minutes. For this reason, you should check the document carefully and add any necessary changes.

- ♦ Therefore, it is very useful to manually save an action, e.g., a table completed or a paragraph written after it has been completed.
  - ✋ Then you can chop off this part of the text and know where to start in case of a crash.

However, this auto-recovery does not replace a data backup. If your hard drive breaks down or you accidentally delete your document, everything including the AutoRestore info is destroyed. Therefore, make regular backups to removable media such as USB sticks or recordable CDs or DVDs.

Note: ....

....

....

....

....

....

....

....

....

13.7 Folder Exercise

➢ **Create** the following folders and sub-folders on a USB-Stick:

➢ **Write** two short letters and **save** them in Letters\Private.

    ↳ No double work: write the first letter, set, save,

    ↳ then only change the text for the second letter and save it under a new name with "Save file as".

> USB stick:
> ↳Letters
>   ↳Private
>   ↳Authorities
>   ↳Apartment
> ↳Study
>   ↳Literature
>   ↳Philosophy
>   ↳Psychology

◆ Once a letter template has been created, it can be used again and again. The same goes for student research projects (or letters, reports, minutes, recipes, etc.):

    ↳ the first text with "**Save the file as**" under a new name and overwrite the text.

    ↳ All settings (title, table of contents, text formatting, style sheets) are applied in this way.

Rename, move or delete folders:

➢ Under the Administrative folder, create a new **subfolder** Tax Office and another subfolder "Tax".

➢ **Move** the Authorities folder from Letters directly to A:\ (cut with [Ctrl]-X, move the folder back and paste with [Ctrl]-V).

➢ **Delete** the 'Taxes' folder.

➢ **Rename** the Literature folder to "Literature of 18th Century".

➢ **Close** all opened programs.

Copy, Rename, Delete:

◆ With which command can you **copy** a file very safely?

    File-S _____

◆ How do I click to **rename** a file?

    _____ - _____ - _____

◆ How do you **delete** a file (three steps)?

➢ Select   File-O_____   or   -S_____   under,   m_____   the   file, then press the [_____] key.

➢ Deletion does not work if the file is still _____ in a program!

➢ Why is it dangerous to delete an **entire folder**?

    _____

Third Part

Language

Page setup, Hyphenation,
Spell checking,
Quick links, Icons

14. Page Setup, Hyphenation

The first steps in word processing are behind us. This is followed by some practical functions, such as page format and hyphenation. The special characters and spellchecking will be introduced in the next chapters.

14.1 Page Setup

Now you have a new text and a blank sheet. The following are some small tutorials with different page settings.

> ➤ Close all open texts, then start a new text and open the Page Setup Menu:

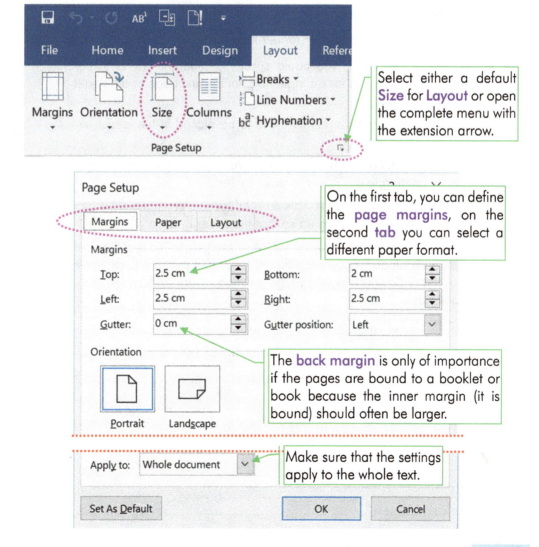

Select either a default **Size** for **Layout** or open the complete menu with the extension arrow.

On the first tab, you can define the **page margins**, on the second **tab** you can select a different paper format.

The **back margin** is only of importance if the pages are bound to a booklet or book because the inner margin (it is bound) should often be larger.

Make sure that the settings apply to the whole text.

The second index card for the paper size:

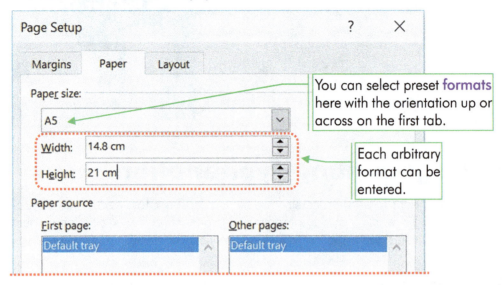

> ➢ Be Prepared:
> Paper size DIN A5 landscape, margins 3 cm each.

> ➢ Always note the preview in the above layout menu.

Preset paper type and print options:

What is explained here is important for longer texts.

◆ Paper feeder: In Word, you could specify a different printer paper feeder for the first page, for example, to print the first page of a booklet on thicker cover paper.

    ↳ The envelope paper would then have to be placed in the feeder selected for the first page.

◆ In File/Extended/Print you will find the Word options with the setting options for printing, e.g., "Reverse print order".

    ↳ This prints the last page first. This is useful for printers that eject paper with the printed side facing up so that the order is correct.

◆ On the page margins tab, you can set "Multiple pages" so that they are opposite each other. This converts the left and right margins to an inner and outer margin which is advantageous if you want to print the front and back sides.

Note: ....

....

....

....

....

....

....

....

14.2 The Hyphenation

The hyphenation of long words and justification is particularly important so that the lines are not excessively drawn apart.

> Word automatically hyphenates the text, but hyphenation must be activated once for each new text.

Write the following exercise text:

Great Cycling Guide of Germany

It is now possible to cycle between Lake Constance and the Baltic Sea. There are 252 cycling tours for single bikes for groups or family outings which are described precisely and the routes are shown in clear and colored map sections.

➢ Then copy the text a few times until there are multiple lines and words that need to be separated using the right indent. You will see that hyphenation is disabled for the time being.

You can select more than just the format for the page layout:

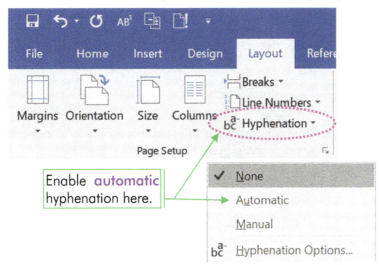

Enable **automatic** hyphenation here.

This menu appears in the hyphenation options:

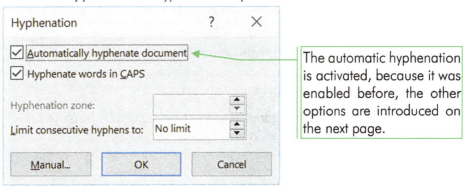

The automatic hyphenation is activated, because it was enabled before, the other options are introduced on the next page.

14.2.1 The Hyphenation Options

♦ **Separate words into uppercase characters**: completely uppercase WRITTEN words are also separated.

♦ The **Hyphenation Zone** determines how small the individual syllables may be. The value must be adjusted for very small or large font sizes.

   ↳ A large hyphenation zone means fewer hyphens but more divergent text.

   ↳ Currently, this function is deactivated which could be changed with every update.

♦ **Successive hyphens**: In books, a maximum of two hyphens should follow each other which can be specified here. Exceptions: very narrow text columns, e.g., in a newspaper.

   ↳ The third line is simply no longer separated and may, therefore, be far apart necessitating a manual check of the separations.

14.2.2 The Manual Hyphenation

♦ The **Manual** Button:

   ↳ Word goes through the separations individually with you. You can accept the suggested separations (Yes), reject them or change them (move the cursor to another position).

Note the marking:

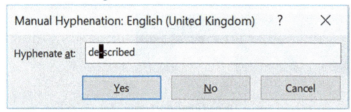

You could use this menu if the automatic function separates words incorrectly or not at all. However, there is a more practical way to do this which is presented on the next page.

> It is necessary to check the hyphenations because some technical terms are not hyphenated at all while others are hyphenated incorrectly.

14.2.3 Separations by Hand

♦ The **conditional hyphen with [Ctrl]-hyphen** is only printed at the end of the line if the hyphen is actually hyphenated!

   ↳ **Therefore, never separate with the normal hyphen**, because you would have to remove these again with text changes!

➢ **Save** the text as a Cycling Guide, then close.

♦ You can specify whether conditional hyphens should be displayed in the **File/Options** and then in the **Display** menu.

15. Spell Checker

You have probably already noticed some red underlined words. This is the automatic spell checker.

15.1 The Principle

- ♦ Word has a Dictionary.
  - ↳ Each written word is compared with this dictionary.
  - ↳ A word that is not in the dictionary will be highlighted.
  - ↳ That's why the red underlined words are not necessarily wrong!
- ♦ This will show you the limits of spell checking:
  - ↳ Word does not know many words, especially for technical texts.
  - ↳ You can add the unknown words to a so-called user dictionary.
  - ↳ Useful for recurring technical words, of course also for your name, street, etc.

15.2 The Automatic Detection

- ♦ Unknown words are underlined in red while writing.
  - ↳ The spell checker can be fixed immediately instead of running over a long text in a marathon action.

Automatic Spell-Checking Exercise:

➢ Write the text with some intentional errors.

Spelling Correction Exercise "Misteke":

This is erroaaaar text with intentionalllly built-in errors. Please write dooown this text with the erroaars or other imaginative errrs in order to then cocorrect these errors. Have looots of fun with it.

Start correction:

Of course, words can also be changed conventionally by deleting the error and writing it correctly. Then you would use the automatic spell checker only for error detection. However, it often goes easier with the suggested corrections.

- ♦ Press the right mouse button on a red underlined word.
- ♦ Correction suggestions are displayed at the top of the scroll list. Depending on the word, sometimes several, sometimes none.

Correction suggestions for "Misteke".

Mistake

Mist eke

Mistaken

Mistakes

Ignore All

Add to Dictionary

Add to AutoCorrect ▸

Cut

Copy

Paste Options:

Smart Lookup

Translate

Link

New Comment

The options:

- ♦ Select the correction suggestion if the correct word is included.
- ♦ If your word is spelled correctly and still underlined in red, Word simply does not recognize this word.
  - ↳ Press "Add to dictionary" to add the word to the user dictionary or press
  - ↳ "Ignore all" so that the word in this text is no longer objected to, or "Ignore" so that it is no longer underlined this time.

- ♦ Click "Add to AutoCorrect" if you want Word to correct this error automatically in the future.
- ♦ The Language menu by Review/Language allows you to change the spelling of foreign words so that the spelling checker works for them as well.

All the options can be found in the Check menu at the bottom of the status bar:

Open the Spell Checker menu.

Change language.

The Spell Checker, Grammar Checker, and AutoCorrect menus are introduced in the second volume.

16. Quick Modules alias AutoText

Repeating texts can be saved and quickly inserted instead of rewriting them.

16.1 Define Quick Modules

Let's say you work for the following association:

> Association for the preservation and care of the association preservation registered the association
> Section, Germany
> Oberkirchner Str. 47 - 33444 Neukirch
> Phone: (1231) 23 12 13 - 0 ◉ Telefax: (1231) 23 12 13 – 223

I understand you don't want to write that name too often. So, we define it as a quick module:

> ➢ Write the club's name once.

> ➢ Format correctly (centered, select font size and font, possibly small caps and color) and then highlight completely.

> ➢ Select "Save selection to Quick Part Gallery" on the Insert file card for Quick Parts.

>> ✎ This option can only be selected if the text to be defined as quick modules is already selected.

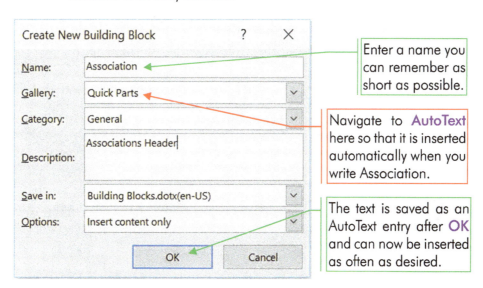

16.2 Insert Quick Modules and AutoText

The quickest Method:

> ➢ Write the AutoText name "merge" and press Return as soon as the reference to the AutoText appears.

Difference between AutoText and the quick module:

- ♦ A quick module is not automatically displayed during writing and inserting with 'Return' but after writing the name, [F3] has to be pressed for the quick part function or it has to be selected from the quick module menu.

  [F3]

  - 🖑 The abbreviation is replaced by the full quick part entry immediately after [F3].

> [Alt]-[F3] to define a highlighted text as a quick module and [F3] to insert a quick module after the abbreviation (the quick modules name) has been written.

> ➢ Add the text again as a quick module instead of AutoText and try to insert it, then delete an entry from the menu described below.

16.3 The Menu

You can see all entries in the "Building Blocks Organizer" menu under Insert/Quick Parts and you can change or delete speed part entries:

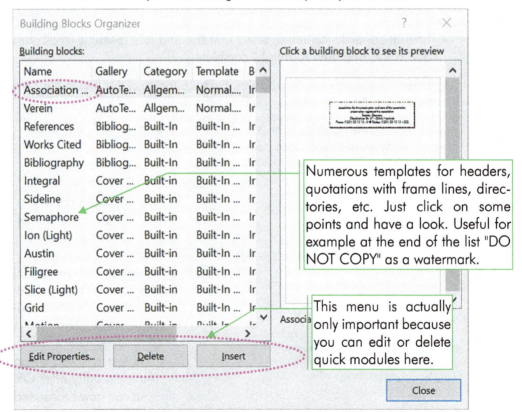

Numerous templates for headers, quotations with frame lines, directories, etc. Just click on some points and have a look. Useful for example at the end of the list "DO NOT COPY" as a watermark.

This menu is actually only important because you can edit or delete quick modules here.

16.4 Another Quick Module

We practice with another text from the practical professional life.

➢ Define the following text as a **quick module** and format it with a very small font.

➢ Assign the name **DelTerms** to the quick module:

> Extract from the terms of delivery and payment: All prices are free domicile plus VAT (domestic) and are subject to change. All offers are exclusively for industry, trade, commerce, and similar institutions. The goods remain the property of *ABC Sample Ltd.* until all previous and future invoices have been paid in full. From a net goods turnover of € 100 of home delivery, with lower order value we raise a small quantity surcharge of € 10. Delivery is made on open account and is payable within 10 days with 2% discount or within 30 days net cash. Place of performance is the registered office of our company. Subject to prior sale, model, color, price changes, and printing errors.

➢ Write a letter with some offers and insert the quick link into this document.

Of course, you don't necessarily have to write the entire exercise text in a course, which should be mentioned here briefly towards the end.

16.5 Quick Modules for Data Backup

Do you sometimes write offers? You can also save your company's products as quick modules.

➢ Save the following text as quick module "**Word2016-2**":

> **Word 2016** training book, second volume, approx. 126 pages.

♦ Quick blocks are saved in the template file normal.dotm, which you can find in **C:\Users\UserName\AppData\Roaming\Microsoft\Templates**.

♦ If you create many quick modules, this file should be taken into account in your **data backup**!

   ✎ Or simply create a text in which you insert all your quick modules, save this text in your default folder, then if you had to reinstall Microsoft Office, you could redefine the quick modules from this text as quick modules.

♦ Since this template file is saved in a different folder for each version of Word, it's best to try finding it in Windows Explorer with the Search button at the top right... and the entry **normal.dotm**.

16.6 Alternatives to the Quick Module

♦ You can save your standard letter once as a sample.

✎ Retrieve this letter for each additional letter and save it again with "Save as". All settings are now available, including the same text from "Dear ..." to "Best regards" including the header and footer with the letterhead and the bank details except for the letter text.

♦ The mail merge function of Word should be used for addresses. Then the addresses are saved in a table (see the second volume).

16.7 Final Exercise

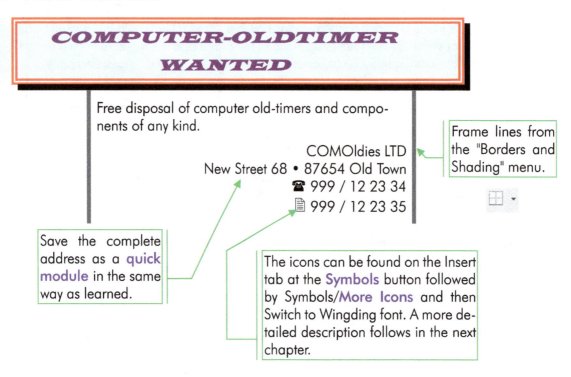

➢ Write the ad, format it with the border lines, and then print it and cut it out.

Notes: ....

....

....

....

....

....

....

....

....

17. The Icons

Icons are special characters that are either not available in the alphabet or not on the keyboard and with which you can make texts more appealing.

17.1 With the US Keyboard

We already mentioned this in the keyboard description on chapter 2.2. Here again for the sake of completeness.

➢ New file with the **paper size** of 10x8cm and 2,5 cm of **page margins**. This signs you can write with usual US keyboard layout:

> the clamps: [the ed.], {Quantity A},
> Two and three high: 4^2, 7^3, 55^{23},
> The Backslash: \
> The pipeline ampersand: |,
> the Spider Monkeys: @
> and the approximate sign: ~

17.2 Acute Accent and Grave Accent

These characters can be created with a usual US keyboard:

♦ Grave accent (à, è, etc.), type ` (to the left of 1), then write the letter.

♦ For **é** or **á** type ' (single quote), then write the letter.

É
à

♦ Others: Circumflex accent (ê), type ^ (shift + 6) then e,
"ö" type " (shift + ') then o,
the Euro € with [Alt]+0128 or [Alt]+0164 and on US international layout: [Alt GR]+5

> Theodor Fontane: Cécile,
> à la Carte, à la jardinière.

More you can find in the internet.

17.3 Insert Icons

There are special fonts on every Windows computer that consist only of images and **special characters** to complete the fonts.

➢ You can activate these icons on the **Insert** tab under **Symbols/Symbol/More Symbols...**

> With the font "**normal text**" you can insert the **Euro sign** or for Eastern European names letters like š. You can also write the € directly with [Alt Gr]-e.

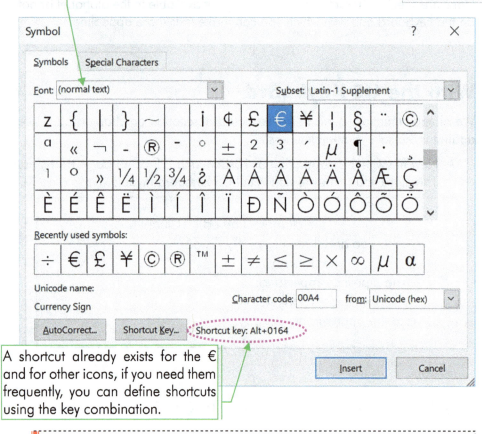

A shortcut already exists for the € and for other icons, if you need them frequently, you can define shortcuts using the key combination.

> You can insert an icon either by **double-clicking** it or by using the "**Insert**" button. The icon is always inserted at the current cursor position.

♦ Every normal font has considerably more characters than shown on the keyboard. Select "(**normal text**)" from the font menu above to use these special characters. This will give you special characters that match your current font.

♦ Special fonts, on the other hand, consist only of images, see Wingding's.

Instructions for using the icon scripts:

♦ Press the arrow for Font.

♦ Use your mouse to click on one of the fonts now displayed.

♦ You can now use the **directional keys** to scroll up or down and display the available icons in the simplest way.

17.4 The Special Fonts

♦ Windows contains several special fonts, e.g., Wingdings (for Windows objects) or Webdings.

♦ Take a look at the beautiful images. A small selection of the characters at Wingdings:

    ✎✂✄✁📖☎✉🕮🖂🖃🖅✆✌✗⌘✠⊠🕭→➤➢↖⇧⇩❑✓🗐

♦ Some other nice fonts may have been installed if you have other programs installed.

> So, take your time to search through your special writings! Different fonts and special fonts can be found on every computer depending on the installed programs.

Exercise special symbols:

➢ Write the following, paper size A5 landscape, 4 cm page margins:

> Hello Janina, ¶
>
> have we already done it ☎today? We're ✈ going on vacation tomorrow and we're certainly going to have a 🖂✎. So, look into the 🖘 and don't always sit in front of the 🖳. ¶
>
>   Bye☺¶

➢ Insert the symbols from the menu "Insert/Symbols/Symbol/More Symbols":

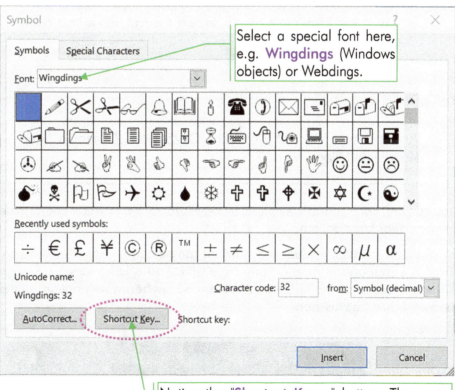

Select a special font here, e.g. Wingdings (Windows objects) or Webdings.

Notice the "Shortcut Key..." button. There you can define a shortcut key if you often need an icon, or check if a keyboard shortcut is already set.

Icon Exercise:

➢ Write this exercise, setting a special page format of 8x6 cm and 2 cm of page margins:

> Oeuvre • © Peter Patent ✈⑤‰ (Per mil) ❀ A Mære is an old fairy tale • Mrs. of Staël • Alexandreïs • 5 £ ❀ ±5% ❀ © Copyright ❀ 4³ ❀ ¼ lbs. meal ❀ ¾ Liter¶

17.5 Foreign Characters

Foreign names are not uncommon in business letters. It leaves a better impression if you spell the names of your business partners or customers correctly.

> This is possible because the standard Arial and Times New Romans fonts include some other characters, such as Bulgarian, Greek, Polish, Russian, Slovenian, Czech and Hungarian.
>
> The Arial Unicode font is also available. Unicode is a font that contains all internationally used letters.

The application in the practice for occasionally missing characters:

♦ Letters like that are written with Times or Arial.

♦ Use insert icons to find the missing foreign characters in these additional fonts "Unicode" and insert them as usual.

   ✇ If you need icons more often, create a shortcut and write it down on a note.

➢ An Exercise. Write with the font Arial:

> Anton Dvořák, Bedřich Smetana, Czyżewski, Żelazowa, Koželuch! Milanovič

You can only write correctly with foreign fonts if you either have an appropriate keyboard or knowledge by heart which letters can be found on which key.

In Windows, an additional language layout can be added at Start/Settings/-Time & Language/Region & Language with "Add a Language", a foreign keyboard layout can be selected at "Advanced keyboard settings" or at the bottom right of the taskbar:

17.6 The Special Characters

Now we come to the second tab at **Insert/Symbols/Symbols/More Symbols**. Here you will find the copyright Icon and Icon for various spacing next to the dash.

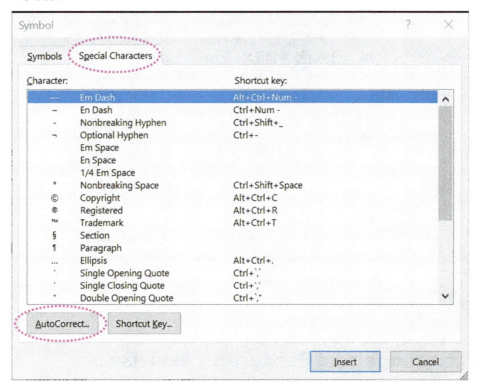

- ◆ The optional hyphen is for hyphenations, the **en-dash** a little longer as the short hyphen (Nonbreaking Hyphen) and the em-dash the longest.

   ✎ **EM Dash** is an old unit of measurement from the time of the mechanical printing set with movable letters.

- ◆ The protected characters, e.g., the **nonbreaking space** or **Ellipsis** are not separated in the case of justification and should, therefore, be used, for example, for information such as $ 20.

- ◆ Also, the **three dots** "..." (Ellipsis) are not separated in contrast to manually written three dots in justification and are not separated.

- ◆ **Em-, En- and quadrilateral spacing** are well-known measurements in letterpress printing: The EM distance corresponds to the font height (= quadrilateral) while the EN corresponds to half the font height. Detailed information on this can be found at **www.wikipedia.org**.

The different Hyphens:

Normal: - [Dash], note: For automatic hyphenation, do not set manually, use the **optional hyphen** with [Ctrl]+Dash (not the "-" by numeric keypad).
Medium: – [Ctrl]-[Minus] ("-" by numeric keypad)   = Compound Words
Long: — [Ctrl]-[Alt]-[Minus] ("-" by numeric keypad)   = Dash

> *Attention! Use the minus sign on the right of the numeric keypad for last two options, the dash for dash and an optional hyphenation.

17.7 AutoCorrect

The AutoCorrect entries are usually used, for example, to automatically replace an abbreviation with the full name. Here you can have the system automatically insert an icon or special text when you enter a character string.

- ♦ Insert/Symbols/Symbol/More Symbols, select the symbol you want to replace automatically, then press the AutoCorrect button, then enter the word to be replaced by the icon:

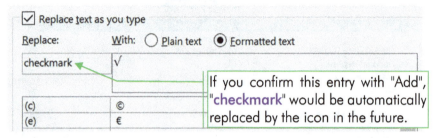

- ➢ Try the example out for yourself. If necessary, reopen the AutoCorrect menu, search for the entry in the list and delete it again.

- ✎ This is the way to get to the AutoCorrect: File/Options/Proofing/-AutoCorrect Options.

17.8 Language and Paragraph Exercise

- ➢ Page size 6 x 9 cm, margins 0,8 cm each, activate hyphenation, write text, pay attention to paragraph marks and new lines! Use long hyphen ([Ctrl]+[Minus]).

- ➢ Format text (font, font size), then highlight the text with the "verbs" and set white columns with 0.6 cm spacing for page layout.

- ➢ Assign the appropriate language to German or English and set the hanging paragraph as shown.

**The principal forms of
irregular verbs[2]**
Irregular Verbs
Irregular verbs marked with an asterisk (*) can also be replaced
by the regularly formed form.

Abide (*bleiben*) – abode* – abode*	**beget** (*zeugen*) – begot – begotten
awake (*erwachen*) – awoke – awoke*	**begin** (*anfangen*) – began – begun
be (*sein*) – was – been	**bend** (*beugen*) – bent – bent
bear (*tragen, gebären*) – bore – getragen: borne – geboren: born	**bereave** (*berauben*) – bereft* – bereft*
beat (*schlagen*) – beat – beaten	**bet** (*wetten*) – bet* – bet*

Fourth Part

Tables

Tabs and Tables for Aligning Text

18. Tabs

Tables and Tabs are required in many documents. Tabs are often unpopular, but wrongly so, as you'll see below.

- ♦ A text can be indented with **tabs**.
  - ✎ The text then stands perfectly and exactly under each other like in columns.
  - ✎ Good for short sections or in the middle of a text.
- ♦ A **Table** (see next chapter) serves the same purpose,
  - ✎ is better for longer text modules because it is easier to use.
  - ✎ Tables can be embellished with table lines.

18.1 Tabs Instead of Spacebars

Many indented the text laboriously and unprofessionally with lots of spacebars. **However, if the text or the font size is changed, everything has to be reset.**

The tabs will convince you to make your text easier to read. Here is the first exercise:

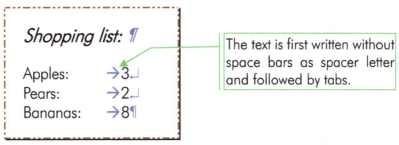

The text is first written without space bars as spacer letter and followed by tabs.

We do not yet need a table for this simple listing. Tabs can be set with the [Tab] key.

- ➢ Write text, placing a tab after each colon with the Tab key.
- ➢ Press **[Shift]-[Return]** at the end of the line for a new line and a new paragraph with Return at the end after "**Bananas: 8**".
  - ✎ All paragraphs would have to be selected to change tabs if you had multiple paragraphs. If you forget to select, the tabs will be chaotic and the settings will be different.

18.2 Tabs Set

Tabs can be set in the ruler located at the top under the icon band if not, switch on with **View/Ruler**:

> ➢ **Set Tabs**: If you click once in the lower half of the **ruler**, a tab will be set here.

> ➢ **Move Tabs**: you can move existing tabs with the mouse in the ruler and move them horizontally.

> ↳ You must remain exactly in the ruler, otherwise delete the tabulator. Make sure that the tabulator remains visible in the ruler.

> ➢ **Delete Tabs**: drag a tab from the ruler to the bottom, then release the mouse button to delete the tab.

> If the **tabs** are not visible in the text, enable them via **File/Options** on display.

Complete the Exercise:

> ➢ We only have one paragraph. That's why it's enough to place the **cursor** in the paragraph to select the paragraph.

> ➢ Press somewhere in the ruler, rather too far to the right to **set** the first tab.

> ➢ **Move** the tab to the left in stages until the order of the numbers is correct.

18.3 Various Tabs

Two parts belong to the tabs. One is to set a **tab character** in the text using the [Tab] key, the other is to set the **tab position** in the ruler.

> ➢ Start a new exercise and write the following text.

> ↳ Set **tabs** with the [Tab] key in the correct places during writing "→" as shown in the illustration:

right-justified	*left-justified*	*centered*	*decimal*
→ Art.-No.	→Designation	→Storage time	→€/Kilo ¶
→ 1001	→Apples	→6 Weeks	→7,89 €↵
→ 1002	→Bananas	→2 Weeks	→14,90 €↵
→ 100356	→Pumpkins	→8 Weeks	→9,90 €↵
→ 100444	→Pepper	→4 Days	→23,67 €¶

Set an [Return] after €/Kilo only when everything is ready, in order to move the tabulator separately for this line.

We have just used the default left-justified tab. Just as a paragraph can be, so can tabs.

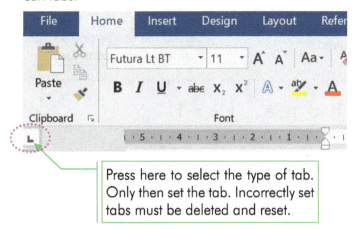

Press here to select the type of tab. Only then set the tab. Incorrectly set tabs must be deleted and reset.

Each click takes you to the next tab:

- ♦ **Left-justified**: the text is arranged one below the other on the left,
- ♦ **centered**: the text is centered on the center of the text,
- ♦ **right-justified**: the text is aligned to the right,
- ♦ **decimal**: for numbers, prices etc., because the comma is always below each other.

More symbols at the tab stops:

- ♦ **Vertical line Tab stop**: this can be used to insert a **vertical line** without affecting the text and tab order.
- ♦ The **first line indent** is followed by an Icon for the first line indent and
- ♦ for the **hanging indent**.
  - ✋ With these last two icons, you move to the respective sliders in the ruler to indent the paragraph.
- ➢ Set the first tab to the right and set it in the ruler. Switch to left-justified, also set, and so on.

| Read the instructions below carefully if you have any problems! |

18.4 Problems with Tabs

- ♦ Tabs can become a problem if there is not enough space between them.
  - ✋ The text does not have enough space and jumps into the next tab field to create **chaos**.
  - ✋ Therefore, it is best to start with links, move this tab until the first column is clearly visible.
  - ✋ Proceed only with the next tab.
  - ✋ It is better to delete all tabs and start again slowly with the first one.

18.5 Two More Exercises

Tabulators are difficult in the beginning but very useful and important and therefore two more Exercises are required.

Set another empty tabulator behind the **telephone** so that the underlining continues.

Telephone list

Name	Department	Tel.
Tember, Sep	Management	233344-4
Ust, Aug	Marketing	2344-122
Mber, Dece	Purchasing	345566-233
Vember, No	Test	7682344-455

The following exercise was set with two right-aligned tabs, see the picture for illustration:

every·Weekday: → 9^{00}·–··12^{00}·Hrs↵

Our Opening Hours:

(right-justified Tab) (right-justified Tab)

every Weekday:	$9^{00} - 11^{00}$ am
additionally Tue, Thu:	$3^{00} - 6^{00}$ p.m.
Saturday from:	$8^{00} - 11^{00}$ am

18.6 Superscripts

The superscript numbers 00:

♦ Mark 00, press right mouse button on it and select font from the drop-down menu and superscript crosses.

♦ It is faster to use the **icon** or keyboard shortcut for superscript **[Ctrl]+**, where the plus to the left of the return key is to be used while the plus on the rightmost numeric keypad does not work.

x^2

↳ Once again **[Ctrl]+** switches back to the normal text position.

Work more efficiently:

♦ You can copy the first superscript 00 with **[Ctrl]-C** and paste it with the next numbers with **[Ctrl]-V**.

↳ Or use the "**Transfer format**" button at the end to transfer the superscript formatting to the other zeros.

You only need to superscribe once with these methods.

19. Tables

Tabs are essential for shortlists in a text. A table is usually more suitable if there are several columns and rows. This is because a table has clear columns and Word can automatically add lines and fill patterns to tables.

19.1 Create Table

➢ We want to create a timetable and a new document, first create some empty paragraphs, then click on the table icon and select some rows and columns in the drop-down menu:

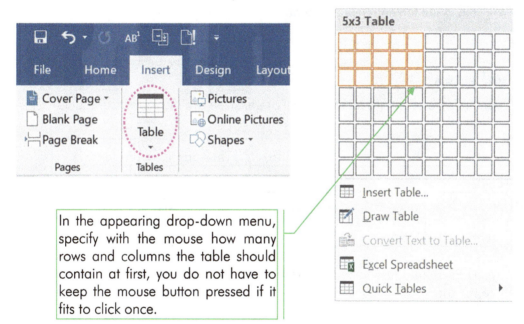

In the appearing drop-down menu, specify with the mouse how many rows and columns the table should contain at first, you do not have to keep the mouse button pressed if it fits to click once.

Create a table with 4 columns and rows and fill the fields (cells) of the table with the following text:

Monday	Tuesday	Wednesday	Thursday

You can access the next field of a table by using the navigation keys, the tabulator key or simply by clicking on it with the mouse.

19.2 Add Columns or Rows

go with the right mouse button, if previously marked correctly.

19.2.1 Add Columns

➢ There is still one column missing for Friday. Let's add a column at the end of the table:

> Move the mouse around the top of the column until the thick marker arrow appears, then press the right mouse button and choose Insert/Insert Column Right from the drop-down menu.

Monday	Tuesday	Wednesday	Thursday	
English	P.H.E	History	Physics	
Physics	Music	Religion	Social studies	
German	Math's	German	English	

➢ Fill in the table further as shown.

19.2.2 Add Lines

There are several options for this as well of which the two most practical should be presented.

Monday	Tuesday	Wednesday	Thursday	Friday	€
English	P.H.E	History	Physics	German	€
Physics	Music	Religion	Social studies	French	€
German	Math's	German	English	Geography	€

> Press the right mouse button to the left of the last row - this marks the row and selects Insert rows below from the appearing drop-down menu.

> Or place the cursor in front of the character at the end of the line and press [Return].

19.2.3 Select Rows or Columns

You can do this in the following ways, all of which you should try out:

♦ Drag the mouse over the whole row or column.

♦ Click once in the left margin at the height of the row.

   ✎ You can also select several rows on the left margin by holding down the mouse button.

♦ Click at the top of the table to highlight a **column**.

 ↳ You can recognize the correct position by the fact that the **mouse arrow** changes to a small arrow ↓, pointing to the column.

 ↳ If you hold down the mouse button, you can select **several columns** or even the entire table.

♦ If you press the **right mouse** button at the correct position instead of the left one, the drop-down menu will be opened at the same time.

♦ If the mouse operation is too uncertain for you, it is more comfortable via the **Layout** menu (only appears if the table is clicked).

 ↳ There you can **select** a row, column or the whole table under the heading Select.

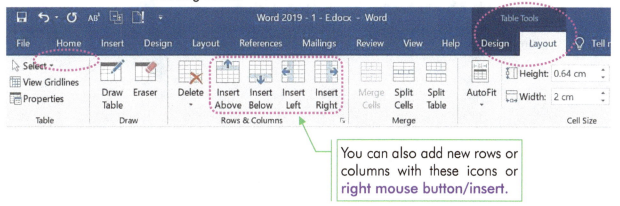

You can also add new rows or columns with these icons or **right mouse button/insert.**

19.2.4 Move Rows and Columns

If a row or column is **selected**, it can be dragged to another position with the mouse.

➢ Select the **Thursday** column.

➢ **Interchange** the Columns Thursday and Tuesday.

 ↳ Correct this again with the **Undo** command.

➢ Drag the **English line** behind the German line, then undo this change.

➢ Add one column for the **time** and two more lines for the subjects.

That's how it should be:

Time	Monday	Tuesday	Wednesday	Thursday	Friday
8^{00}-8^{45}	English	P.H.E	History	Physics	German
8^{45}-9^{30}	Physics	Music	Religion	Social studies	French
9^{30}-10^{15}	German	Math's	German	English	Geography
Break					
10^{45}-11^{30}	Math's	Physics	Biology	German	Physics
11^{30}-12^{15}	Biology	English	Math's	Math's	English
12^{15}-1^{00}	French	German	English	French	

19.3 Embellish Table

The table is completed in the Shell. Word has some very nice **table templates** that you can assign.

➢ Place the cursor in the table and go to the **Design** change tab:

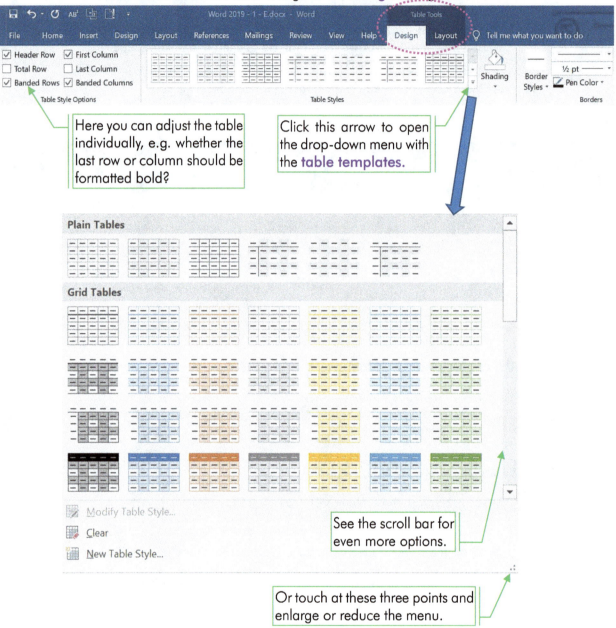

Here you can adjust the table individually, e.g. whether the last row or column should be formatted bold?

Click this arrow to open the drop-down menu with the **table templates.**

See the scroll bar for even more options.

Or touch at these three points and enlarge or reduce the menu.

➢ Go through the formats, then assign a suitable **table design**.

   ✎ The result will be displayed in the original table as soon as you let the mouse rest on a template.

➢ After assigning a template, the table can be individually embellished by selecting the desired rows or columns and then formatting them with e.g., **Borders and Shading**.

   ✎ Only the default setting could be adjusted in the above menu with Change table format template, whereby there are only a few setting options in the menu that appears.

19.3.1 Adjust Column Width

In the Layout menu, you will find at the AutoFit option with these choices in the drop-down menu:

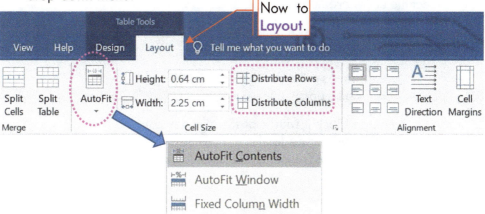

AutoFit:

- ♦ The first option adjusts the column width to the contained text. The columns will be reduced as much as possible.
  - ✍ Even if several cells have already been joined, this function can still be used because the joined cells are not compressed.
- ♦ The table is set to text width, i.e., extended to the edge of the page, with "**Automatically adapt to window**".
- ♦ **Fixed column width**: the column is not fixed, i.e., you can still change the column width manually with the mouse,
  - ✍ but if you enter longer text, the column width will not be adjusted automatically, but the text will be split,
  - ✍ similarly, inserted images are only displayed up to the edge of the column.

Spread Rows or Columns:

- ♦ **Spread Columns** distributes the columns so that each column has exactly the same width.
  - ✍ The entire width of the table is not changed.
- ♦ Similar to the above, the effect is to **spread lines** with a vertical direction only.
  - ✍ If, for example, one row has several columns, the other rows receive the same height, even if they only contain one row.
  - ✍ The entire height of the table is changed if multi-column rows exist.

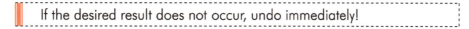

If the desired result does not occur, undo immediately!

Adjust Column Width Manually:

Move the mouse over a column border and as soon as the mouse arrow changes to a double arrow, the column width can be adjusted individually by holding down the mouse button.

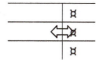

19.3.2 Connect Cells

The break line is to become a huge field:

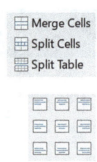

> ➢ Select the entire break line.

> ➢ Select Connect right mouse button cells or the icon in Layout.

> ➢ For the break line, set the paragraph orientation to center which is also possible for layout.

> ➢ Select Break and lock it with 9 pt (Start index card and the extension arrow for Font followed by the extension arrow for Advanced), then set it to bold.

The result is a long break line:

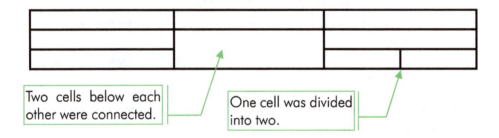

930-1015	German	Math's	German	English	Geogra-
– Break –					
1045-1130	Math's	Physics	Biology	German	Physics

Other Options:

> ♦ It is also possible to connect cells below each other if the cells or the whole column have been selected before! This is also possible with the command "Connect Cells".

Two cells below each other were connected.

One cell was divided into two.

The reverse way is possible with table tools/layout/split cells. It even asks if you want to split the cell into multiple columns or horizontal rows.

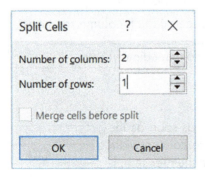

19.3.3 Format Colored Table

⧗	MONDAY	TUESDAY	WEDNESDAY	THURSDAY	FRIDAY
8^{00}-8^{45}	English	P.H.E	History	Physics	German
8^{45}-9^{30}	Physics	Music	Religion	Social studies	French
9^{30}-10^{15}	German	Math's	German	English	Geography
10^{15}-10^{45}	🔔 Break 🔔				
10^{45}-11^{30}	Math's	Physics	Biology	German	Physics
11^{30}-12^{15}	Biology	English	Math's	Math's	English
12^{15}-1^{00}	French	German	English	French	—

Procedure:

➢ Make the table appealing with **table format templates**.

➢ The **column width** can also be adjusted manually with the **mouse**.

> Each row or column can then be **changed manually** by selecting it and selecting either **Shading** or **Frame Types** from the Table Tools/Draft menu.

19.4 Additional Settings

19.4.1 Define Table

You can set all table values, such as row height or column width by right-clicking on the table and choosing **Table properties**.

> If you want to set specific areas, e.g., only one column, select them beforehand.

The following four index cards can be set in this menu:

♦ Index card **Table**: the orientation of the entire table.

   ✎ The table can also be moved with the mouse at the top left of the box.

   ✎ Here you can activate **text wrapping** for a table so that the text continues to run to the right or left of the table, see an example on the right.

Table	

Table Properties:

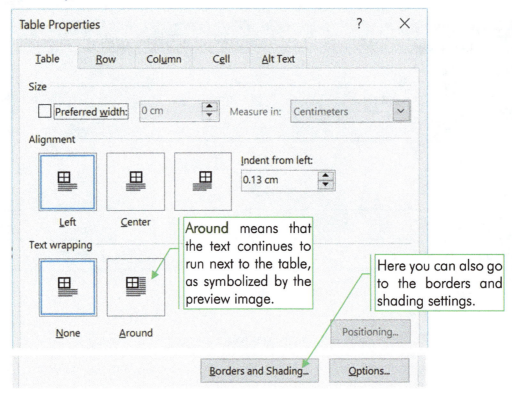

The row height or column width can be specified exactly for the **row** and **column** index cards. This is sometimes useful if you know exactly how wide a column should be.

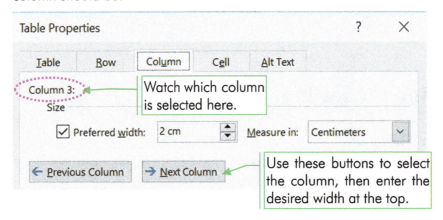

19.4.2 The Text Position

♦ The vertical alignment of the text can be determined on the penultimate cell index card.

It is often better to center the Text vertically in Tables.

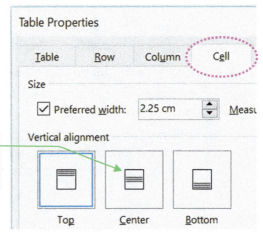

These settings are hidden at the bottom of the cell menu under Options:

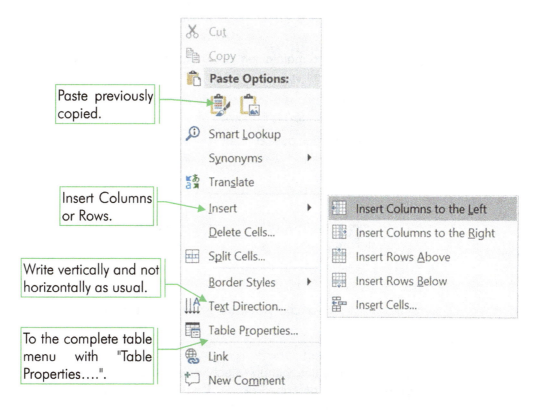

Wrap text: text is automatically continued in a new line as soon as the end of the cell is reached when writing and the table cell is increased accordingly.
Fit text: the font is stretched so that it occupies the entire cell.

A text can be entered on the last **Alternative Text** index card that appears as an alternative to the actual text if the table is still being loaded on the Internet or cannot be loaded correctly. This index card is therefore only of interest if a table is to be published on the Internet.

19.4.3 Additional Input Options

Almost all-important settings can also be accessed by pressing the right mouse button on the table.

Paste previously copied.

Insert Columns or Rows.

Write vertically and not horizontally as usual.

To the complete table menu with "Table Properties....".

The appropriate commands will be displayed depending on what was selected.

19.4.4 Timetable Exercise

➢ Create a new exercise table with the following text:

Schedule

	Date 02/04/2022	Time
Monday	Visit to customer Donald Donaldson because of Fan Shop	8^{00}-9^{30}
	Visit to Customer Micky Mick due to print dates	10^{00}-11^{30}
	Visit to Customer Daniel McDan due to Patent takeover	14^{00}-15^{30}

➢ Format the table as shown.

➢ Then try to get similar results with the quick tables: Insert/Table/Quick-Tables. If not possible, undo afterward.

19.5 Problems with Tables

The following is a common cause of errors in tables:

♦ The paragraph setting is set to a spacing before or after the paragraph.

    ✎ This spacing is also maintained in tables, so that the text may not be centered but moved upwards or even cut off.

♦ Since the usual text settings also apply in a table, an exact line spacing can be the cause if the text is truncated after enlarging the font.

    ✎ The same effect can cause a fixed row height in the table properties.

Correction:

♦ Select text, open the paragraph menu on the Start tab with the extension arrow at Paragraph, there

    ✎ reset the spacing before/after to 0 pt and the line spacing too simple.

    ✎ If this does not help, check the settings for table properties.

> However, a paragraph spacing is a very good method of fine-tuning the height of a table line. Simply select the whole table, then go to the paragraph menu as described above. Please note, if you want to reduce the distance again!

19.6 Tabulators and Tables Exercise

Note: first open the header with Insert Header and complete the first exercise there. Perform the second exercise in a new file. Once the header is open, double-click to navigate between the header and the text.

19.6.1 With Tabs and Line

> Create the following Letterhead, first with Tabs:

Tab left	centered	right
OVERALL, TO	BOARD:	LONG STREET 33
STUDY	DR. CHARLOTTE SAMPLE	88888 MUNICH
THE LANGUAGE	PROF. DR. EGON WORD	PHONE: 089 / 33 33 33
IN THE TEACHING		TELEFAX: 089 / 33 33 34

Note: see Insert/Shapes you find lines, vertical or horizontal lines can be drawn with the [Shift] key pressed.

19.6.2 As a Table

OVERALL TO	BOARD:	LONG STREET 33
STUDY	DR. CHARLOTTE SAMPLE	88888 MUNICH
THE LANGUAGE	PROF. DR. EGON WORD	PHONE.: 089 / 33 33 33
IN THE TEACHING		TELEFAX: 089 / 33 33 34

> Create a three-column table in the header row, write text (either with a new row or in new table rows), left-align, center-align, right-align,

> Select the table, set the line below for right mouse button frames and shading but invisibly for other lines (grid lines).

19.6.3 Add a Text at the bottom of the Footer

BANK DETAILS	REGISTERED ASSOCIATION	MUNICH DISTRICT COURT
BANK 11223	DONATIONS TAX	PR NO. 4566 666
SORT CODE 345345345	DEDUCTIBLE	PLACE OF COURT IS MUNICH
CT.: 123444		

> Complete the letter template with header and footer as well as the text "Dear Ladies and Gentlemen", which is always required,

> then save it in a "Business Letters" folder and print it.

19.7 Page Setup Exercise

Create the following Sticker for a Jam Jar.

Plum Jam

homemade

from fresh, especially sweet plums. Preserved according to an ancient home recipe.

Country of Origin: Grandma's Garden
Minimum shelf life: 11.2021
Ingredients: Plums, Sugar, Lemon juice, Rum.

Unattended snacking strictly forbidden!

> With tabs possible or as a table by hiding the table lines after completion.

The special features of this Exercise:

➤ Set the paper size to approx. 9 cm wide and 6 cm high.

➤ A frame around the whole page with beautiful Pictures would be of course very suitable (see p. 60).

➤ Select attractive font and font color.

➤ Printing is done on self-adhesive labels or normal paper, which is then cut out and glued on.

To Paper Size and Printing:

The possibility of printing on labels is described in detail in the second volume of the chapter on serial printing. These simple possibilities for the time being:

◆ You can specify that two or more pages should be printed on one sheet for file printing on the left.

✎ Or cut through a DIN A4 sheet beforehand and print on DIN A5.

Fifth Part

In Conclusion

WordArt, a Letter, the Help

20. WordArt Special Effects

♦ Special effects such as in a graphics program have long been possible in Word with the WordArt function:

↬ Text with Shadow, Shading or with spatial Perspective always in color!

And the Best: the operation is very easy. That's why it's more about relaxation and a relaxing chapter at the end of this book.

20.1 Start WordArt

➤ Start a **new file** and create some empty paragraph marks there. You will find the WordArt icon on the **Insert tab** near the Quick Parts:

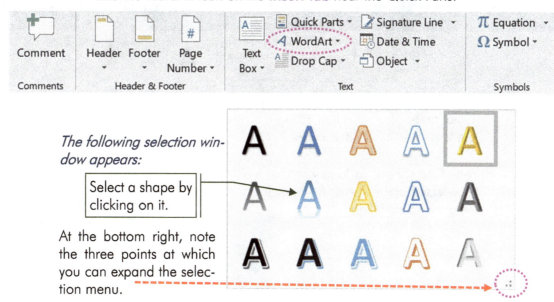

The following selection window appears:

Select a shape by clicking on it.

At the bottom right, note the three points at which you can expand the selection menu.

➤ **Select** the desired shape and enter the desired **text** in the window that appears, e.g.:

The text can even be **rotated** with this lever.

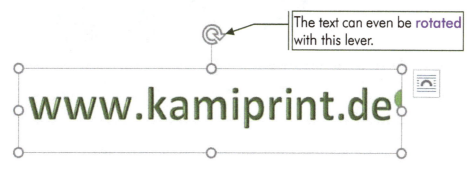

www.kamiprint.de

Ready! The result rotated slightly and with fill color:

www.kamiprint.de

> Because WordArt requires a lot from the computer, you should only use it for a few words and not for longer texts!

20.2 Set WordArt

Each preselection can be set individually.

♦ Like any graphic, you can **move** this object with the mouse or change the **size of the handle points**.

♦ The object can be edited again as soon as you click on it. Especially interesting are the **drawing tools**:

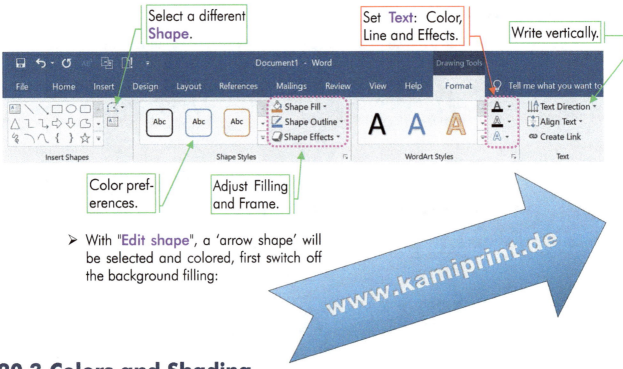

Select a different **Shape**.

Set **Text**: Color, Line and Effects.

Write vertically.

Color preferences.

Adjust Filling and Frame.

> With **"Edit shape"**, a 'arrow shape' will be selected and colored, first switch off the background filling:

20.3 Colors and Shading

> Note that you can also open complete menus with the **drawing tools** using the small **extension arrow**:

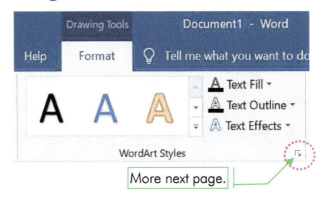

More next page.

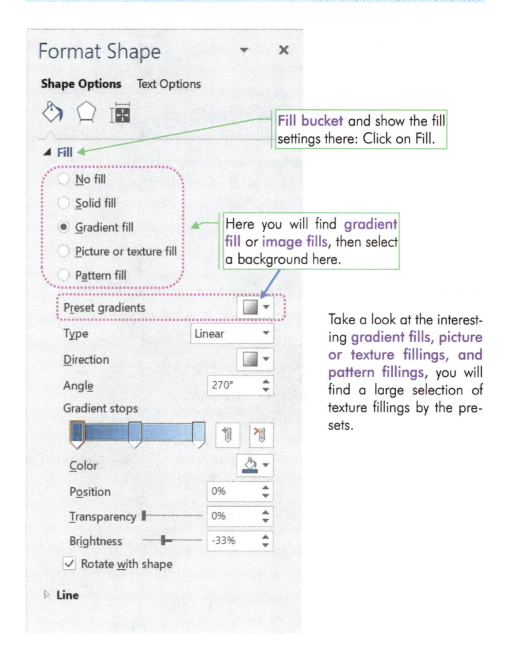

Fill bucket and show the fill settings there: Click on Fill.

Here you will find **gradient fill** or **image fills**, then select a background here.

Take a look at the interesting **gradient fills, picture or texture fillings, and pattern fillings**, you will find a large selection of texture fillings by the presets.

With color gradient for the text and filling wood for the background:

- ◆ Additional effects can be applied to the background with each filling effect, e.g., a luminous border or shadow or 3D-formats.

- ◆ Any image can also be used as a background for **Image** or **Texture fills**.

20.4 WordArt Exercise

Use your knowledge to create an ad:

> The Text Shape can be changed for **Text Effects/Transform**.

will do

any kind of paperwork for money:

> Lock text by 5 pt.

43333 Overthekeys
Phone: (234) 45 3445

20.5 Mirror and Rotate WordArt

Graphics? with WordArt super simple.

➢ Write and format the following text with WordArt:

First Street 123 ☑ New York

➢ Here a self-made **gradient** was used for the background by setting additional color points with double clicks, for which color was then selected.

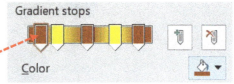

➢ The text was mirrored downwards with **text options**.

Texts can also be rotated for text effects/transforming:

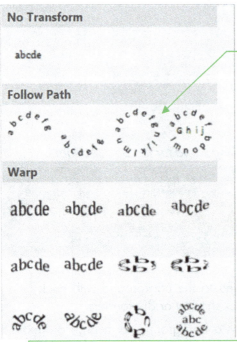

> Try some **perspectives** that others occasionally explore for themselves. You can even arrange text in a circle with WordArt!

First Street 123
New York

> For the text was used a wave 3E-effect, the shape as a banner and the address is set in a rectangle, switch of filling and line after finished of this.

21. A Letter

The first steps in word processing are behind us. This is followed by a real **business letter**, which we can, of course, embellish with a WordArt logo.

➤ New File, DIN A4 with **2,5 cm Page margin** each, or use your favorite letter size, dimensions you find by www.wikipedia.com.

The completed letter should look similar to the one shown:

Walter Sample ☺ Broadway 333 ☺ 98543 Sample City
Phone: 467 / 467 67 00 ☺ Fax: 467 / 467 67 11¶

¶
¶
¶
¶

Walter Sample ☺ Broadway 333 ☺ 98543 Sample City ¶
Albert Smith↵
Air Street 30↵
81999 Nether¶

Sample City, March 28th, 2019¶

Dear Mr. Smith, ↵
Thank you very much for your interest in our fully electronic freezer with automatic speech recognition and deep sleep saving mode as well as night muting and Internet connection including automatic refill. ¶

Child protection deep compartment with output protection, removal counting device, and automatic door closing are standard features. ¶

According to your telephone inquiry, I will inform you about our current quantity discounts for wholesale. ¶

Refrigo Blather RB 3998		
Quantity	Price	Discount
1 to 3	1,389.-	0 %
4 to 10	1,156.-	20 %
11 to 100	956.-	40 %

plus 19 % VAT and shipping fee of 20 €¶

With kind regards ¶
Walter Sample

21.1 Sales Brands in Stock

Useful for every new Text:

- ◆ You have a blank sales mark.
  - ↳ Their settings are quickly changed.
  - ↳ Therefore, use [Return] to create some blank paragraph marks to keep the original settings in stock.
- ◆ Make sure that the Print Layout view is turned on, and
- ◆ choose a favorable zoom level, favorable is page width or on large monitors from 22" two pages.

21.2 The Letterhead in the Header Line

The Header is an area at the top of the page that cannot be changed when editing the text and is automatically printed on each additional page.

That's why the header line is very well suited for a letterhead which should be printed with every new letter unmodified as if we would print on already pre-printed letter paper. The same applies to the footer line, in which the bank details are often placed, for example, in a letter, and the page numbers are usually found in a book.

- ➤ Select the Header button on the Insert tab, then the top empty header to open it for the first time.

- ➤ Write your address or the sample address with the WordArt icons and logo as letterhead in the header:

Walter Sample ☺ Broadway 33 ☺ 98543 Sample City ↵
Phone: 123 / 4 67 67 00 ☺ Fax: 123 / 4 67 67 11¶

- ➤ Format the text as follows: left-justified, small font with 11 dots using a different color.

- ➤ Insert the arrow as AutoForm, add a gradient and place it behind the text (right mouse button in the background).

> Once the header has been opened, double-click on the text area to navigate to it and double-click on the header to reopen it. Attention! If you subsequently select a different header preset for the Header button, the existing text in the header is deleted. Possibly. copy the text first, change the header, then copy the text back.

More about the headers and footers follows in the second volume of MS Word, such as how to insert page numbers or how to set up different headers.

21.3 The Address

➢ The distance between the letterhead and the address is simply generated with a few **empty paragraph marks**.

➢ Copy the **sender** from the header and format it nice and small: **8pt, left justified, italic, underlined**.

Walter Sample ☺ Broadway 333 ☺ 98543 Sample City ¶

➢ Below is the address:

Albert Smith ↵	_[Line feed Shift-Return]_
Air Street 30 ↵	_[Line feed Shift-Return]_
81999 Never¶	_[Paragraph mark with Return]_

➢ The line breaks make it **a paragraph** from "Albert Smith" to "Never". Please adjust as follows:

    ✎ left-justified with one and a half line spacing and font size 12 pt.

21.4 Insert Date

Next comes the date.

➢ Write Right Justified:

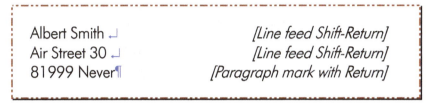

Sample·City,·March·28th,·2019¶¶

Just go with it:

➢ Insert File card, Date and Time:

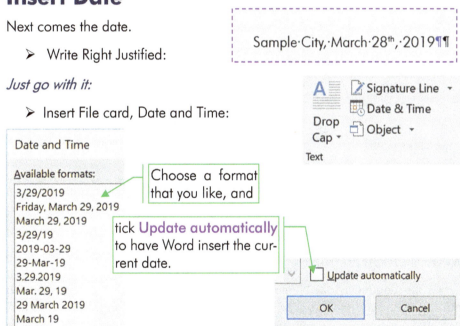

Choose a format that you like, and

tick **Update automatically** to have Word insert the current date.

Information about the automatically inserted Date:

◆ With the next letter, you will use this as a template and save it under a new name with **Save as**.

    ✎ Address changed, text slightly adjusted, already completed, after printed and **incorrect date**. To prevent this from happening to you, Word can be prompted **to update** the inserted **date** each time you print.

> You should not use this function if you want to recheck the date later, for example, for **invoices**.

21.5 The Letter Text

➢ You can now write the text as shown on page 109.

  ✎ Leave the line break to the computer, just press Return at the end of a paragraph!

Notes on the Settings:

➢ Please still **write** and adjust the table.

➢ Format the text as follows: Font: 12 Points, Paragraph: Line spacing 1.5 lines, Spacing before and after Paragraph: 6 pt.

➢ It is essential to enable automatic **Hyphenation**!

The Ending is still missing:

> plus 19 % VAT and shipping fee of € 20 ¶
>
> With kind regards ¶

➢ **Right-justified** and small format with **7 points** font size

➢ **7 Points**? You cannot select this font size from the list, but you can enter it in the font size selection window:

  ✎ to select the entire line,

  ✎ then write 7 in the font size selection window

  ✎ and confirm with **Return**.

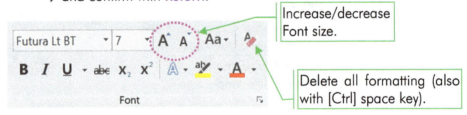

Increase/decrease Font size.

Delete all formatting (also with [Ctrl] space key).

21.6 The Footer

Open the header by double-clicking, then simply click on the Footer at the bottom and enter the usual text, such as a bank detail, e.g., with a **right-justified tab**:

HOUSE BANK, MUNICH	SAMPLEALBERT LTD.
SORT CODE 11 22 33 22 11	LEGAL VENUE IS MUNICH
CT. NO.: 66 55 66 77	

21.7 New Letters

Open it with every **new letter**, make a copy by **saving** it as a copy and only change the text and address which is a much easier method than with the document templates.

21.8 Letter by DIN

We have compiled the most important rules from DIN 5008 (German Industry Standard) for business correspondence herein.

- ♦ In a new document, set the left margin to 2.41 cm, the right margin to 2 cm and the bottom margin to 2 cm in accordance with DIN standard 5008.

  - ✆ You could enter the Letterhead in the Header line to protect it from unintentional changes.

  - ✆ Then you would enter **Layout for the header 1.69 cm** and **4.5 cm** for the sender as top margin on the Layout tab.

- ♦ Use small font and separator to specify the sender address above the area for the address, so that the letter can return if necessary.

The correct Address:

To one Person:	To a Company:
1. Shipping form	1. Shipping form
2.	2.
3. Salutation, Title	3. Company
4. Name, Company	4. Department
5. Street, P.O. Box	5. Contact Person
6.	6. Street, P.O. Box
7. Country code, Postcode and City	7.
8.	8. Country code, Postcode, City
9. Country	9. Country

2,41 cm | 1.69 cm

The Construction:

Letterhead with Sender
(1.69 cm from top)

Sender's details slightly above the address ....
This address block must fit into the window of
the envelope; therefore, it should be 4.5 to 9
cm high and 8.5 cm wide.

4.5 to 9 cm

Your message from   Our message from   Extension, Name   Date (reference character line)

Reference line without "Subject"

Dear Sir or Madam,

Letter text, clearly formulated with blank lines for structuring.

With kind regards (including signature)

Attachment(s): (if available)

Detailed information, as well as templates with dimensions (Form A and Form B), can be found at **www.wikipedia.de**, where you can search for DIN 5008.

International are various letter formats and writing rules usual, you find in the internet descriptions and examples four your country.

21.9 Preview

The second book will deal with longer texts:

- This is why the style sheets are helpful which can be used to format long texts rationally.
- And for longer documents, a header line, page numbering and a table of contents should not be missing.
- Many practical functions are also covered, e.g.:
  - Search and Replace,
  - Multiple Columns,
  - advanced Table Features,
  - how to set up new Icons or Keyboard shortcuts,
  - Insert Images as well as the Feature in Word to draw etc.
- Then it's time to print Serial Letters, Labels, and Envelopes.
  - This feature is also included in the second volume because serial letters and labels also require the use of a database, where it can be discussed thoroughly with many exercises.

The third book* is dedicated to Professionals,

or for those who want to become one. Word can do almost everything like a good computer typesetting program.

- Here you can learn how to create Brochures, Club Newspapers, Advertising Documentations or Real Books with Word.
- It is no problem to insert any number of Images, Tables, Graphics or Columns.
- Typographical standards such as kerning or living headers are also feasible with Word.
- In the third volume, we will also add a keyword index and
- for a perfect, print-ready appearance of the documents, explain how different headers or footers can be set up in a book or exercise book.

Designed special Editions for MS Word:

- Serial letters, Labels, and Envelopes with MS Word.
  - These topics are dealt with in detail in the second and third volumes. All the material is compiled in the special edition and supplemented with additional exercises.

Chapter

22

22. Index

A

Acute accent 79
Adress block..........................78
Alternative text......................99
AutoText........................ 75–78

B

Bold....................................20
Border............................57, 60
Bullet..................................56

C

Caps....................................23
Cell......................................91
Centered 27
Close 18
Color 57
Column................................91
Condensed............................50
Copy....................................29
Correct................................11
Cursor............................11, 33
Cut 29

D

Date insert............................111
Delete 14
Dictionary............................73
DIN 113
DIN A5................................70
Document template 77
Documents 17, 34, 64
docx....................................17
Double click..........................33

E

Effects 30, 48, 60, 105
EM Dash 83
Exercise
   -Announce 78
   -Birthday Invitation 41
   -Border 57
   -CD Insert 37
   -Design............................30
   -Error text 11
   -Folder 66
   -Font settings................ 19–24
   -hanging paragraph............53
   -Headline............................50
   -Hyphenation 71
   -Language and columns 84
   -Letter..............................109
   -Letterhead........................101
   -Numbering 56
   -Paragraph settings 27–30
   -Plum Jam..........................102

-Poem.................................52
-Quick modules..................76
-Schedule........................100
-Scroll bar.........................44
-Spell checker....................73
-Stroller.............................38
-Supermarket....................20
-Symbols...........................81
-Table...............................91
-Tabs.........................87, 88
-Telephone list..................90
-WordArt.........................106
Exit....................................18

F

Felt marker 21
File 15–40
  -Save as..................... 63–64
File-Options.........................26
Fill effects.........................107
Filling 57
Folder
  -Overview 17, 64
Font 23
  -Adjusting..................... 19–24
  -Adjusting = Formatting........19
  -Design..................... 47–51
  -Effects...........................30
  -Font size 112
  -Install 51
  -Size...............................22
  -Superscript.....................90
Foreign fonts 82
Format Painter.....................51
Formatting
  -Font 21
  -Formatting characters..........26
  -Paragraph.................27, 28
  -Reset 21
  -Styles...........................114
Frame 59
  -Adjust line.......................59

G

Grave accent 79
Gravure..............................30

H

Header........................ 110, 114
Highlight 21
Hyphen 83
Hyphen, conditional...............72
Hyphenation 71, 72

I

Icons............15, 32, *See* Symbols
  -Icon bar 34
Ident 52
Insert..................................29
  -Date and time 111
Intend 56
Internet..............................114
Italic 20

J

Justification...........................27

K

Keyboard.................. 12, 13, 14
  -Delete 14

L

Language settings...................82
Layout.................................36
Left-justified..........................27
Letter.......................... 109–12
Line 60
  -New................... 13, 14, 25
  -Spacing 28
Listings 55
Lock...................................50

M

Mailings 7, 8, 78
Mark................................19
Mouse...............................33
  -Right button.......................23

N

New line.............................13
normal.dotm 77
Numbering 55

O

Open 39
Overview 119
  -Copy.............................44
  -Delete.............................14
  -Folder.......................17, 64
  -Font settings 23
  -Keyboard 12, 14
  -Paragraph settings..............28
  -Save.............................63
  -Word editions 7, 114
  -Word functions......................8

P

Page
  -Border 60
  -Page width 41
  -Setup............................70
Paper size 70
Paragraph
  -Alignment 27
  -Hanging 53
  -Ident............................28
  -Indentation..................54, 55
  -Intend............................56
  -Line spacing 28
  -Numbering......................55
  -Paragraph mark...............25
Print 61–62
Program bar.......................31

Q

Quick modules................. 75–78
Quick Tables.....................100

R

Repeat................................29
Right-justified 27
Ruler 55
  -On/Off 54
  -Sliders 55
  -Tabs 88

S

Save 15–40
  -Save as...................... 63–64
Scroll bar.......................35, 43
Serial letters 114
Shading..............................58
Shortcut...................... 12, 114
Small Caps 23
Spacing..............................50
Spell checker................... 73–74
Status line.......................31, 36
Structure..........................107
Styles .... *see* volume two
Superscript..........................90
Symbols................... 15, 79
  -Foreign..........................82
  -Insert.............................82
  -Symbol fonts 80

T

Table........................... 91–100
Table of Content..................114
Tabs.......................... 87–90
Template............................36
Text
  -Adjusting ....See Font
  -Design............................47
  -Intend............................56
  -Mark 19

-Move 20
-Open 39
-Save 17
-Scroll 43
-Switch 40
-Where save? 64
-Window 34

U

Underlined 20
  -double, wavy... 24
Undo 29

V

View 36
  -View type 31

-Whole page 41

W

Webdings 81
Whole page 41
Window 40
Wingdings 81
Word
  -Close 18
  -Start 11
  -Structure 34
  -View type 36
WordArt 105–8

Z

Zoom 41

Note: ....
....
....
....
....
....
....
....
....
....
....
....
....
....
....
....
....
....

23. Overview

Start, Window, Cursor:

- Start-Programs-...,
- Background/Fullscreen/Exit,
- **Format** = Set Text,
- first click or select,
- Delete with [Back] or [Delete] key,
- **Adjust** Words:
    - select with a double click, undo.

Open and save Files:

- for **File**: New, Open,
  as Icon: Save,
- save in **folder** + subfolder clean up,
- to a suitable backup medium, e.g., removable hard disk, at regular intervals,
- **File extensions** from Word:
    - docx = document = Text (formerly doc),dot = document layout = Document template,
- and select [Delete] to **delete**,
- Double click starts, double click with a pause allows you to **rename** files or folders.

Formatting: **F *K* U** · ab̶c X₂ X²

- either **icon** at the start, the extension arrows for complete menus, or
- right mouse button on the desired Text followed by the appearing toolbar.
- **Font**: Font type or size, CAPITAL LETTERS or SMALL LETTERS, double underlined, color
- **Paragraph**: Line spacing, spacing before or after, indent left or right, change alignment, etc.

Layout, Hyphenation, Spell Check:

- **Layout**: Paper size, Margins ...
- the **Hyphenation** can be found in Page Layout Hyphenation,
    - [Ctrl]-[dash] for the manual hyphen,
- red underlined words = automatic **spell check**: right mouse button to correct or add.

Print

- **Print** with [Ctrl]-P; for print or file printing:
    - **Printer properties**: adjust this,
    - **Settings**: Set Word.

Useful Effects:

- Insert **Icon** or with [Alt Gr]: 5^2, @, [], {} or with accent: é è,
- special **Fonts**: thick Fonts, Manuscripts,
- **Lock/Compress** on Start Font Extension Arrow on the Advanced tab,
- Numbered Paragraph, **Enumeration**, Indent at the start by means of these icons:

Frame and Shading:

- Select "**Borders and Shading**" at the bottom of the **start frame icon** in the drop-down list.
    - Or select one of the presets directly at the frame icon, e.g., to set only one line on the left side instead of a complete frame.
- Text can be highlighted in color on the **Shading** file card.
    - Do not choose a color for inkjet printers but rather a percentage color value of approx. 20%, otherwise the color and the text will fade.

Set Word:

- **File options** for setting Word,
  - the storage location for documents can be preset for **Save.**
  - Assign shortcuts for Customize Ribbon.
  - The **Quick Access Toolbar** can also be added to icons here.

WordArt, transferred, Tables:

- **Transfer Format:**   🖌 Format Painter
  - once transferred click once with an icon
  - or with a double-click on the icon repeatedly.

- **Quick modules:**
  - Write, select, insert Quick module selection ... save or [Alt]-[F3] so that the entry is saved,
  - Write start, confirm with [F3].
  - Or as AutoText, so that the suggested text is displayed automatically when you write.

- **Tabs:**   ⌊
  - always start on the left,
  - in the ruler, move, delete,
  - left-aligned, centered, right-aligned, decimal or vertical.

- **Tables** (for Insert):
  - with Insert **Icon,**
  - Select **Row** or **Column,** right click on it and add, move or delete,
  - Preset or design manually with frame and shading,
  - **Sort** by name, date, etc. by clicking on column header.

- **WordArt:**
  - with the icon in the Insert menu,
  - and modify it using the WordArt toolbar.

Letter:

- Insert **Date** and Time,
- Set letter as a template once, then always copy with **Save as** and only change the text.
- Letter according to DIN address fits into the window of a DIN long envelope.

Copy, Delete, Rename in the Start menu:

- use **[Ctrl]-X, C, V** to cut, copy, paste, or icons,
- select and [Delete] to **delete,**
- These shortcuts and [Del] can be used to **rename, copy or delete** files when opening or saving a file:
  - Double-click starts, double-click with a pause to **rename** files or folders and [Delete] deletes the selected file.

Standard-Shortcuts:

[Ctrl]-n	New Text	[Ctrl]-x	Cut
[Ctrl]-o	Open Text	[Ctrl]-c	Copy
[Ctrl]-s	Save	[Ctrl]-v	Insert
[Ctrl]-p	print		
[Ctrl]-z	Undo	F1 or ?	Help

Some more Keys and Shortcuts:

Keys:

[Esc]	Escape: Escape, Abort without change, ideal emergency button.
[Back]	Delete to the left.
[Del]	Delete to the right.
[Alt], [Ctrl]	Special keys for abbreviations, e.g. [Ctrl]-s for saving.
[Alt Gr]	^{2} ^{3} { } [ ] \ | @ ([Alt Gr] not available on US keyboard)
[Tab]	Tabs for indenting text.

Paragraph and Line:

[Shift]	Write uppercase letters.
[Return]	New Paragraph.
[Shift]-[Return]	New Line in same Paragraph.
[Ctrl]-[Return]	Insert Page Break.
[Ctrl]-[Space bar]	Resets font settings to their default values.

Move in Text:

[Ctrl]-[Pos 1]	To start with.
[Ctrl]-[End]	To the end of the text.
[Ctrl]-g	Go to.
[Ctrl]-f	Search (f for locate).

Select with a pressed mouse or with the keys:

[Shift] -Direction keys -Image keys	Select (from the current cursor position). The selection can also be reduced by holding down the [Shift] key.
[Ctrl]-[Shift]-[Pos 1] / [End]	Highlight from the current cursor position to the beginning or end of the text.
[Ctrl]-A	Select all.

Hyphenation:

[Ctrl]-dash	Manual Hyphenation.